Twice Alive

A Spiritual Guide to Mothering Through Pregnancy and the Child's First Year

Beth Osnes

ISBN: 0971938385 *306,874*
LCCN 2004115999 *083*
10,1D

With honor and love I dedicate this book
to my mother, Dorothy Claire Beehner,
whose compassion, faith, and vision have lit my way.

Contents

Introduction   ix
Chapter One: The First Trimester   1
  What to Watch For   1
    Just Starting Out   1
    Secrets   2
    Swinging in Euphoria   3
    Swinging into the Dark Side   3
    Finding Your Place in the Creative Process 4
  One Traveler's Journal   4
  Something To Do   13
    Start a Birth Journal   13
Chapter Two: The Second Trimester   17
  What to Watch For   17
    Balance Restored   17
    Entering the Public Domain   18
    Be Fabulous   19
  One Traveler's Journal   19
  Something To Do   23
    Design Your Own Baby Shower   23
Chapter Three: The Third Trimester   31
  What to Watch For   31
    Leaving Cute Behind   31
    Rev your Engines   32
    Rare Vista   33
  One Traveler's Journal   33
  Something To Do   41
    Arrange for Your Meals When Baby Comes Home 41
Chapter Four: A Possible Over-due Contingency   45
  What to Watch For   45
    Enter Misery   45
  One Traveler's Journal   46
  Something To Do   49

Chapter Five: Birth 51
  What to Watch For 51
    Forever Changed 51
  One Traveler's Journal 52
  Something To Do 58
    Get the Word Out That You Need Some Recovery Time ... 58
Chapter Six: Infanthood (0-3 Months) 61
  What to Watch For 61
    Re-entry into Your Life 61
    Falling in Love 62
    Guarding this Time 62
    Girl Talk with God 64
  One Traveler's Journal 64
  Something To Do 79
    Create a Prayerful Place for Yourself 79
Chapter Seven: Age of Opening (4-6 Months) 83
  What to Watch For 83
    Step Slowly from your Cocoon for Two 83
    Dive into the Deep-end of This Love 84
  One Traveler's Journal 85
  Something To Do 96
    Celebrate your Shared Sensuality with Baby 96
Chapter Eight: Age of Discovery (7-9 Months) 101
  What to Watch For 101
    Premonitions of the Separation to Come 101
    Grace Descending 102
  One Traveler's Journal 103
  Something To Do 120
    Join or Form a Mom's Group 120
Chapter Nine: Leaving Babyhood Behind (10-12 Months) ... 127
  What to Watch For 127
    What is Gained and What is Lost 127
    Rebounding Acceptance 128
    Seeing Double 129
  One Traveler's Journal 129

Something To Do   140
    Spread the Love to All the World's Children   140
Chapter Ten: Epilogue (The End of the Beginning
and Beginning Again)   149
    Conclusion: Eight Years Later   149
      As Foster Mother   150
      As Political Mother and the Creation of Mothers Acting Up   153
      Mothering as a One-Woman Show   157
      The Graduation of a Birth-mother   162
      Adoptive Mom   166
    An Apple a Day   176
Footnotes   180
Photo Credits   181
Something to Do (pages to fill with notes, insights, ideas)   183

Introduction

Expect to feel well-loved by this book, mother. Expect to be cared for and encouraged. My hope is to draw your attention to all the spiritual wonder within as you multiply yourself times two. As a fellow traveler who has loved this terrain, my desire is to point out amazing vistas, to share your enthusiasm and magnify your own with my affirmation. This book is here to lend a hand when you stumble, firmly demand you watch out for yourself, and ensure that you reap the most from this great soul-harvest called *birth*.

As you embark on this journey through procreation this book travels with you, chapter by chapter, beginning with the first trimester, through pregnancy and a possible "over-due contingency," to birth, and through the first year of the child's life. Each chapter welcomes you in by introducing the subtle or, sometimes, the screaming nuances of each particular phase, lovingly encouraging you to look for the particular gifts of each development and supporting you through the challenges. The "One Traveler's Journal" section is the bulk of each chapter and reads as journal entries from that time during the birth of my daughter, Melisande. My intention here is to spark the dialogue of stories about mothering among mothers through the sharing of my stories. All the best gems of insight are buried beneath a mountain of circumstances and can only be mined through the telling of the entire tale. For us mothers, the lessons are embodied within the experience. As a chance to get out and stretch your legs along your travels, there is a suggested "to do" at the end of each chapter especially suited to the terrain and advantages of your particular place along this journey. Practical, memorable and adventurous, these "to do" outings are supported with clear and easy directions to make them both fun and rewarding for you.

The goal of any travel is more than to survive getting there; it is to gain perspective, richness and connections along the way. Traveling into procreation is all this and so much more. It is a chance to reach unprecedented intimacy with your partner, a chance to micro-travel into the intricacies of life itself, and a challenge to your endurance, patience and courage like nothing else. Procreation is your hook into the most essential act of humanity and your ultimate justification for taking up part of the world's oxygen supply. Having a baby is a chance to fall so deeply in love as to thrill at a blinking of your baby's eyes. It is your purchase of a stake in the future and your reason to plan for it. Brace yourself for the journey of a lifetime and expect to arrive completely transformed.

This book is not a "how to" nor does it give instruction on how to mother, rather it sits beside you as a friend on a tour boat pointing out glorious waterfalls as well as dark hidden places of beauty. As a comfy companion, it shares the intimate internal experience of mothering that is seldom talked about but deeply felt. It challenges you to think more about and get more out of this mothering experience at a time when it is most intense, fresh and demanding. This book is a celebration party for your graduation into a higher being. It is a companion who understands. Most of all, it is my attempt to validate the bounty of spiritual awareness and wisdom gained by mothers during pregnancy and the first year.

Within journal accounts, I reserve the right to be wildly contradictory in my feelings; warm and aglow one day, nihilistically pondering the parasitic growth within me the next. Pregnancy and the first year are a roller coaster of extremes in both pain and ecstatic joy. I reserve the right to flagrantly change writing styles, from personal and intimate to scholarly and philosophical. Mothers are all this. They are not just fuzzy and cute, but sometimes babies make them feel very fuzzy and crushingly cute. They are still as smart and inquisitive as they were before being pregnant; it's just that now their punch bowl has been spiked with hormones and they have another passenger on board. Sometimes they have a sense of humor about being the birthing parent and sometimes they don't. That's just how it is, so literary standards of conformity of style will just have to relax or, God forbid, expand to include an accurate documentation of the "childed experience" for women.

While speaking of this pregnancy I, naturally, compare it to previous pregnancies. Allow me to give you a quick rundown. First off, at the age 20, I was a birth-mother to a beautiful boy child, Ben, who was adopted by my much older brother and my sister-in-law. Since I'm the youngest of a big family, I received a lot of help from many siblings in making a success story out of this unexpected pregnancy. This birth-son was my love child with my French boyfriend, Luc, who I still love dearly but did not choose to marry. Ben's doing great. Yes, he knows I'm his birth-mom, as he says "My aunt's my mom and my mom's my aunt." Yes, I see him pretty often. No, it's not weird. Actually, it's a delicious yet shy love affair. Carrying and giving birth to him cleared out my heart and my ambition at a pivotal time in my life.

Years later after I married JP I had our first child, Peter, my car-seat philosopher. He's a dream of a boy. This was when I had the "first child" experience, even though, as I've just told you, he wasn't technically. Other than teaching a college class and having a contract to write a book on acting, I was and still am a stay-at-home mom, relying on a few college-aged girls and my terrific sister-in-law for baby-sitting. In the beginning with Peter I had the fussy-child-experience where it was a lot about me—wanting to be the perfect mother and to be perceived as such. Not the whole thing, but enough that I cringe a bit on some memories, such as acting like it was a personal affront to receive a gift that wasn't 100% cotton. A lot of us remember being here. It's painful, let's move on.

The next child I bore was a daughter, Melisande. On this one I threw all delusions of "Mother of the Year nominations" out the window and honestly witnessed her unfolding, tuned into her and what the mothering thing did to me and my understanding of *everything*, a subtle inner journey. I was intentionally aware of the spiritual gifts that came my way. *Twice Alive* is based primarily on my writings from my pregnancy with her and the first year of her life.

In the writing of this book, I attempt to be inclusive of all kinds of mothers, married, unmarried, or lesbian. Thus, when speaking in generalities, I refer to a partner rather than a husband. This book is intended for the woman giving birth to a single child since I can't presume to know the unique passage of a woman embarking on twins, triplets or beyond! Though this book is about spirituality, it does not limit itself to any particular faith. My own background is Christian, but I have traveled far in my life and studied much, so I will use influences and examples from many faiths. I do not use the male pronoun to refer to God so some of the prose might sound a bit strange to the reader. I intend no disrespect when I refer to God as "it;" and credit my use of that vague pronoun to the limitations of our English language. Though father images of God have a beauty all their own and summon nurturing associations to be savored, I want to leave God open to more comparisons than that. A major strength beneath this entire work is the discovering of the mother-like qualities of God (and visa-versa), such that the masculine pronoun for God suits neither my experience nor this work.

The spiritual insights gained through mothering cannot be accessed directly nor reduced to a few statements; they are deeply embedded in the actual, day-to-day adventure of gestating, birthing and nurturing. This time in a woman's life stands out as being exceptional and, if attended to with a listening spirit, can be a time of great spiritual awakening. She is in such close proximity to the ultimate creative spirit that she can feel its hot breath on the back of her neck. Is this God benevolent or using her towards its own means? Is she cared for, even loved by this God-force? Is there an inherent goodness in the drive to perpetuate our species? These are the questions that burn to be answered as her being is consumed by procreation. Motherhood is the purifying furnace by which our toils, frustrations and heartaches are transformed into wisdom, compassion and fulfillment. Motherhood is a process through which we are crafted, shaped and, finally, finished by our ultimate creator.

In the doubling of yourself, you have doubled your everything. A child is in the world who is flesh of your flesh, soul of your soul. Though not identical to you, save for the same arch in the nose and long skinny toes, more oxygen is being used up since you procreated. Now you have twice a stake in the future. You have twice the reason to care about the legacy our generation is handing down to the next and twice the strength to make a difference. You have twice the accomplishments to cheer, twice the obstacles to conquer, twice the shoes to tie, twice the laughter and twice the tears. Nothing will ever be as carefree again nor will you likely suffer from lack of purpose. Having reached the highest summit of human achievement, you are sharing your prize with the world in hopes it greets your child with goodness. Seldom used adjectives such as "magnanimous" are being dusted off and placed in sentences preceding your name. If you feel twice as deeply and soar twice as high then, indeed, you must be twice alive.

Chapter One
The First Trimester

What to Watch For

Just Starting Out

Welcome you surefooted travelers! Welcome you frightened friends, you hopeful hearts! Welcome all to the accelerated life-lesson journey called motherhood. Traveling this journey will assure that you be changed forever, expanded, enriched, depleted and renewed both physically and spiritually. Word to the wise: drink it all in deeply. Let it overflow in you. Absorb enough of this immortal drink to last you through that long road ahead.

Part of this leg of the journey might occur without your certain knowledge that you are even on the path of procreation. As you unknowingly stride through your day, little doubts, sudden fears, and tiny hopes might wisp by you, giggling in secret delight, and whisper almost inaudibly, "What if you are? You could be!" If you're hoping for a pregnancy, you might not dare to unleash your excitement. If you're not even thinking about it, you may get broadsided by the very thought. If you decidedly do not want to be pregnant, you may feel as though your hopes, plans, and life are being pulverized by a blender at the possibility of pregnancy. Personally, I have experienced each one of these entrances into pregnancy, and I wish to bear witness to the fact that, in my case, they all eventually lead to an irresistible thrill at the very thought of there being a new life growing inside. Take a deep breath, give in, and let go.

Secrets

In these first few weeks, even months, pregnancy often enters the domain of secrecy. A privileged few—mates, mothers, or sisters—may be invited in to either conspire or commiserate with in private. Nothing is certain at this point, no test or adherence to the uterine wall trusted implicitly. Little signs are watched for: tender breasts, mood swings, a late period, and all are duly noted in your mind's secret calculations. Urges to tell everyone you meet and rack up dollars on your long distance bill are wisely suppressed. My dad used to joke about people who told too soon as "calling from the bedpost." Then there's always the slight risk of an early miscarriage and the misery of having to retell people that actually you aren't pregnant as you thought. No, secrecy, in this rare instance, seems to be the best choice.

This private time is the perfect opportunity to mindfully turn inward and attend to this new idea of your self as a woman with child. You are suspended in time between being a woman and a mother, no longer what you were, but not yet what you will become. This is a time to prepare, both inside and out. It's easy to go out and buy a car seat, borrow a crib, and be the recipient of hand-me-down baby clothes. It takes more effort and focused attention to fully reap the invitation pregnancy brings to join the creative force running deep beneath the surface of the earth that forces up mountains and leads a raging river down its course. Like a belly garden or a human nest, pregnancy can make you feel your connection to all living things, as though creation has confided its secret to you and you carry it inside among an unknowing world.

Swinging into Euphoria

Anticipation can rush through your veins like an injection, like an inhalation of pure excitement. Other prospects that life may hold up—trips, jobs, school—dwarf to the size of peanuts in comparison to the enormous potential of the new life within you. You can feel so honored to be chosen worthy of being entrusted with this child's life and well-being. There is nothing ordinary about you now. You glow. You have a stake in the future and will live beyond yourself. You hold within your belly the explosive potential of a new human spirit.

Swinging into the Dark Side

Conversely, your body can betray your excitement and, instead, fight this new invasion of life. At the introduction of new hormones, nausea creeps in and spreads its gloom throughout your body. At the same time, your body is drained of its energy, now needed for procreation, leaving you fatigued and sprawled on your back over the couch. You may even start to feel a separation between yourself and your child, perhaps, even a rivalry for resources. Deeper still, you may begin to question the very idea of this life-force regenerating itself through you. Assumptions of goodness in God and the beautiful design of life are questioned. You can begin to feel downright used by nature. When regarded through the selfish eyes of misery, this baby can come to be thought of as a parasite in extreme moments. "My God-given libido tricked me into this!" you may shout. Nature seems like a bulldozer fueled by a blind drive to perpetuate the species, and you the crumbling dirt pushed forwards by its brute force.

3
~

Finding Your Place in the Creative Process

This tumultuous questioning can unearth some profound insights into the nature of creation and the force behind it. Your perspective on God is literally inverted since you are now regarding its creative spirit from the inside out rather than the outside in, as everyone else mostly experiences it. Now you not only have awe for creation, you are awesome. You need not only try to wrestle your mind around these ideas of God and creation, you are nearly God-like and a physical co-creator. Your skin, veins and blood are intermingled inextricably with the ultimate creative force. As with any intimacy, questions of love emerge. Like a child with its mother, or a new lover with a partner, you seek reassurance of love. You may ask, "God, do you love me? It seems to matter a bit more now that we're, well . . . so intimate. Do you?"

One Traveler's Journal

May 6

I will write an account of this sensation I believe to be conception, fully knowing that I run the risk of error. As I sit nursing my one-year-old boy reading the book, Moby Dick, I feel an unbalanced nausea creep up my torso. It buzzes under my chin, and then works its way up the back of my head leaving caffeine-like jitters through the bones in my legs. The scope of my vision distorts and reduces. As I take in a breath the air mixes with this new impulse in my tummy. As I exhale the uncertainty is spread through my body. Like a bird soaring upwards out of a blinding mist, my spirit glistens with hope. Blood drains from my upturned face. Swallows feel dry, void of saliva. My buttocks feel full of gravel.

May 19

Self-conscious of being so obsessed about this hoped-for pregnancy, I don't speak of it, but inside, my mind is abuzz. A few months back I talked to my husband, JP, about maybe trying for another baby, that maybe this was a good time. He hemmed and hawed and mentioned overpopulation and other such worldly woes as he scrambled to find an excuse. I know beyond a doubt that he loves having our son, and, in my own presumptuous way, even believe he wants to have another. It's just that some reactions are obligatory to the sexes; men are supposed to drag their feet when women want to have more babies. It's not the absolute rule, but it is the norm. The result of that discussion, as it applies to our practical life now, is that we don't use birth control, not that we were very good with it anyway, but he hasn't really come right out and declared himself as wanting another baby. There's that icky feeling we women can get when we feel as though we are tricking men into parenthood, as if we dangle our sexuality as a lure into the trap. Then I rush to my own defense, "He's a very smart man, and I think he knows where this unprotected tumbling will most likely lead. You're not tricking him. You stated your desires honestly." But in my heart I feel a slight deceit because I am witnessing myself obsessing on having a baby more than I reveal to him, keeping it from him, who is my soul mate and eternal confidant. I'm a little embarrassed to be so premeditated about it all.

The truth? Every applicable sensation I feel is registered and scrutinized as being proof of pregnancy or reason for possible disappointment. On my trip home to visit my mom in Wisconsin, I am seated in the plane with Peter on my lap. As the flight progresses, my stomach churns and tightens in the most unpleasant ways. Having Peter wiggling and needy of my attention is almost too much. I can't pass him off to any other kind faces seated around me because he would cry bloody murder. Seated next to me is a modern-day cowboy with his Stetson politely off his head, resting upturned on his lap. The nausea worsens as we begin our descent. I emphatically ask the stewardess for a cup of ice to suck on to keep the nausea at bay, and hide my stash when the flight crew makes their final check for cups and trays. The hollow cavern of that Stetson seems to be taunting my considering vomit out of me. "No! Down! Relax." I convince myself. Luckily we land before I erupt. "Hmmm," my mind thinks smiling, "last time you got sick on a plane was when you were pregnant with Peter."

At my mom's I am aglow to be with her. I don't speak to her of my suspicion that I might be pregnant, since I seriously lack proof and I don't want to be, as my dad used to say, calling them from the bed-post with the news. My period should be coming this day. Final proof would be either trickling down on its way or not. That night as I slept with my mom in her big king-sized bed, Peter sleeping between us, I dreamt over and again of waking up with gushes of blood flowing out from between my legs, of strawberry stains on young girl's smocks, of dropping a beautiful vase with the flowers, water and broken glass all mingled at my feet. But when I really awoke, all was white and dry. Still, I kept silent with my new secret folded up and stashed deep in my pocket. When I returned home I told JP that I had missed a period and thought I might be pregnant. My worries of JP's willingness were wasted, as my better self knew. He smiled and hugged me to him tightly, his hand gradually moving over to my belly dreamily.

May 22

At times when the chemical balance in my body spills to the side of excess, my insides feel carbonated as excited bubbles unleash a secret thrill inside of me. My hands jitter. Concentration vacates whatever task is before me. The wind breathes life into me, and I am twice alive.

May 22

Life force

As I lay on the couch after a day of kid watching, writing, cooking, cleaning dishes, laundry, and a book project meeting, I feel the exhaustion of living while reproducing. I wonder how much of my intention, my will, is directing the formation of this child. Obviously, I am not the brain behind this project. This being has cells dividing and a design emerging that I don't even understand, let alone control. I am the energy source, the protective shell, and the temperature regulator. This baby will continue growing without any conscious effort on my part. The design is in the egg and the sperm, and all I need is a healthy libido to bring the two together. To borrow a metaphor from Kahlil Gibran's poem in *The Prophet*, there is a life force like an arrow that is being shot from me. I am that bow from which it will be thrust by life. Wondering, I ask, "What is the will of life? What does this life force want besides continuous momentum? Does this life force care for me? Does it care for me?"

May 23

Last night JP rented the movie *Alien 3* for us to watch after Peter went to bed. Clearly, this movie along with *The Fly* (in which a woman gives birth to a maggot in her dream) should be on the top of the "Movies *Not* to Rent for Pregnant Women" list. This movie is bleak from beginning to end with a creepiness that gets under your skin. Our heroine, Sigourney Weaver, crash lands on a penal colony inhabited by twenty-five inmates who have formed a sort of monastery-like, Christian cult among themselves. She, being a woman, albeit one who has to shave her head due to a propensity towards lice on this prison island, is an object of great interest and temptation to their vow of chastity. As the action progresses, we learn that a truly nasty alien has stowed away on her craft and also survived the crash. With serpent-like jaws, the teeth of a tyrannosaurus rex, squid-like tentacles, and more mucus dripping from its nose than an entire class of preschoolers, it usually appears moments after some hapless character bends down to examine some slimy residue on the floor and then the alien devours the poor sucker. Suspecting foul play, Weaver's character gets an ultrasound and discovers she has been implanted with a baby alien. We watch on the ultrasonic screen along with Weaver as she gets a glimpse of junior, jaw and teeth distorted, but without a doubt, an alien. Next we get a close up of her face as this reality sinks in. We register her horror in finding that she carries a beast within her, a parasitic invader, kin to her mortal enemy that gave her more than a hard time in the first two *Alien* movies. Unsavory memories of the first *Alien* movie come to mind, one in particular in which, amid a splattering of fake blood and gallons of ooze, a baby alien comes busting out of a man's chest. My visceral response to these bombarding images is one of utter disgust and near nausea.

At this point, I am most profoundly done with this movie and turn it off. Turning my head towards JP with a "what the hell were you thinking?" kind of expression on my face, he laughs and says he must have had a screw loose when he chose this one. That night in our dark bedroom, still stuck in the gray, gloomy world-view inspired by the movie choice, my awareness turns towards my own pregnant belly. Not only am I entertaining unreasonable fears that this might be an alien implant rather than a human baby, I am struck by my repulsion towards this movie's slimy alien race and its blind drive to reproduce. Then I look at myself and ask, "And how are you so different?" How is my birthing more noble? Are I and my offspring not devouring the resources of this planet with flagrant neglect for the impact we are having on the rest of the earth's creation? Am I not a monster to an anthill that I causally tread upon? Don't all questions of good and evil eventually come down to good being subjectively defined as what is beneficial to my survival and evil being that which opposes it? Then how can I declare the perpetuation of my race as good and the alien race as evil if it's just a matter of perspective (human versus alien)?

This brings me to the larger question of evil. Is there a source of evil out there with its own volition? Growing up Catholic, horrific images of fiery little devils were painted in our young minds. These nasty little fellows were tempting us to shoplift from the candy store or to wear our sister's new sweater to school without asking. As I've grown, I've come to accept what I think of as a more mature understanding of evil—that evil doesn't exist on its own as a viable force, but is, rather, the turning away from goodness, the void of goodness. The makers of *Alien 3* don't seem to agree. Here the force of evil has a viable form, a form that, it just so happens, is a manifestation of most human's worst nightmare. However, as horrifying as this alien race is, there's something strangely comforting about believing that if there is evil, that evil has a root source that is outside of the self. Most of the world's mythology seems to reinforce this view. This medieval portrayal of the human soul being pulled upon by good and evil forces is the simple story upon which *Star Wars*, J. R. R. Tolkein's sagas, and more are based. In this victim-based perspective, I do not have to look inside at the fluctuations in my human heart that chooses selfishness over giving, comfort over growth. I don't have to completely own my actions that may hurt others, because it could be just a lack of starch in my soul that led it to be overtaken by the dark force. I find myself, as I age, grow bored with this medieval, overly simplistic view of the human condition. I don't believe that we as humans are outside the struggle, being acted upon by greater forces of good and evil. I think we are the struggle. More profoundly, I think that we are such stuff that struggle is made of, that the struggle is all within us, and that it spins out into the world from us. My mind flashes on an image of Shiva as Nataraja dancing in a circle of flames—Shiva, the Indian God of destruction from which creation emerges. Yes, we are the human and the alien, and we dance in the flames as one entity.

May 24

The other night it seemed very important to me that this life force that is surging through me care for me. This morning I think that whether it cares for me or not may not be the point. A force doesn't seem emotional one way or the other. It seems the nature of God, the life force, is hiding from us, yet, ironically, is in us. Each cell in my body knows how to repair itself and perform its given function. My body's knowledge is likewise hidden. I do not know how my punctured skin repairs itself. Indeed, I do not need to know for healing to occur. I must say I feel a little miffed, left out, sore. I, in my brain where I seem to be stuck, don't even know God as well as some stupid little white blood cell racing through my veins. That doesn't seem right.

May 28

All I have to do is lower my chin, close my eyes, and feel inside towards the tiny being dividing and multiplying its idea of itself. This being, so much less experienced than I, knows how to become itself without question, without me. Who is leading this child by its new budding hand, drawing the human form out of a miracle of cells and life energy? I walk along side this creative force creating this child. The journey brings me an intimate acquaintance with creativity. At times I feel at one with it, and at times almost used and left out. Sometimes I feel like I have the force and that it is all in me, or, perhaps, that I am made in its design.

June 1

About the life force caring for me

It seems that all of life's truths that I know most intimately and believe most fervently, I know through witnessing the microcosm of a macrocosm. Pondering this, my thoughts turn to the East and the exotic play of shadows in the villages there. During grad school when I was in Malaysia on my Fulbright year, I remember taking a boat and then a bus to Hamzah's house five days a week for him to teach me how to perform the *Wayang Kulit* shadow puppets. In his humble little house built on poles so the monsoon rains wouldn't sweep it away, he would guide my hands as I grasped the carved rawhide puppets. With just a boombox blaring the *gamelan* music that I had recorded at another shadow puppet performance, I would start to feel the power of bringing the great tales of the Hindu gods to life. The white monkey Hanuman demanded strong and robust movements to show off his amazing strength, while the noble prince Rama required decorous and refined movement befitting someone of such high rank. And, of course, I learned to manipulate the leaf shaped *kayon* puppet with its gorgeous design of a tree carved into the rawhide and painted meticulously. This is the puppet I would start each lesson with, as I swayed it back and forth in rhythm to the music in front of the screen to start the show, just like the opening of a curtain in the west. There was something undeniably trippy about the visual effect of this puppet's shadow being projected onto the muslin screen. Images of animated drug movies from the 60s come to mind. Hamzah said it aroused the appetite of the audience for the medium of shadow play. Beyond that, I felt my spirit and mind get aroused and attracted to the imagery of this puppet in motion.

The *kayon* puppet (the design of a tree within the shape of a leaf) is a continuous visual reminder that the wisdom contained within the whole of the story is contained within even its smallest parts. Here the whole story is represented by the tree, and the smallest part by the leaf. Even though a shadow puppet performance lasts from sun down to sun up, only a few of the many episodes in the *Ramayana* can be performed. It would take weeks to perform the entire epic. The audience never experiences the entire tale in the span of an evening. Yet, through the visual image of a tree contained within the shape of a leaf, the repeated presence of the *kayon* puppet reminds the audience that the wisdom of the whole is imparted to them through even its smallest part.

The idea of this *kayon* puppet, which is also called the "tree of life," stirs me deeply. If the wisdom of life is present within the smallest manifestation of life itself, then I turn to you, little leaf in my womb. Unfurl your tender green leaves for me to see. Tell me what I yearn to know. "Does the life force care for me?" It does not answer directly. I lean back in my chair and think. I care so very much for this life growing inside me. It seems hardwired into my very being that I would. Then, I reason, this fetus is like a leaf on my tree and I am like a leaf on God's tree. This little being will be largely created in my image, with allowances for minor cosmetic difference. Thus, if I care so very much for my leaf, and if we (like the baby to its parents) are created in God's image (an idea touted by many religions), then wouldn't it stand to reason that I am cared for even more fully than my babe since the love is coming from a bigger tree, a larger life source? The lushness of this imagery and my conclusions please me very much. It matters very much to me that I am cared for. Though not a proof, for I'm sure any freshman philosophy student could punch fist-sized holes in my logic and refute my premises, it feels like something in which I can believe. Furthermore it feels intuitively true, in concordance with what I have learned in my journey through life. Cool shade from those strong reaching branches, rich with foliage, relieves my burning worries. Take comfort, mother, you are deeply cared for.

June 3

Yesterday I got an official test of pregnancy and the prognosis was positive. The certain knowledge seems to have undammed the surging flood of hormones that were kept at bay by cautious uncertainty, and are invading my body, leaving me exhausted and queasy. Just now, I don't feel "twice alive." More like "half alive."

June 5

Mean as mud
and mad at this nagging nausea.
I feel hesitant, reticent, gloom.
Ukk is emanating from my center.
My body is revolting against this tiny innocent invader.
They will find an equilibrium, but when?

June 7

Last night I told JP that I felt like biting the head off of a dog. Constant immersion in a pool of nausea will do that to a woman. My body is raging against this change, and the headquarters of the revolt are in my stomach. Shall I whimper on the couch, or throw myself into a concrete wall? Relief, where are you?

June 15

It seems that the human tendency to resist growth and change, at the onset, is perfectly manifest in the body of a newly pregnant woman.

June 30

At two months and a few weeks, peace is descending as misery dissipates. I feel perfectly right where I am inside myself with a babe glowing from me.

❦   ❦

Something To Do

Start a Birth Journal

"Who? Me?" you may ask while backing up shaking your head, "Oh no, I'm not a writer!" Au contraire, mother, you are. This is not to be compared against other Pulitzer Prize-winning books; this is a work of love just for you. Photographs capture the outside appearance of memories, but to remember the internal experience and the wisdom gained from them, there is nothing quite like a testimony from your own hand.

Getting Started: Options abound! Just pick one that suits you and your life best or devise your own.

❖ Go buy an extra wide three ring binder in a color that pleases you at an office supply store. Pick out some sturdy unlined and/or lined paper to put into your binder. Then buy some clear plastic, three ring binder, 8½ by 11 envelopes, about ten or twenty, into which you can slip photographs or newspaper clippings.

❖ Purchase a bound journal in book form, one that fits in your bedside table drawer for you to write in before going to sleep each night.

❖ Label a manila envelope "Birth Journal" and place scribbled thoughts you write on paper napkins when waiting at a restaurant, bits of paper on which you wrote out all the possible baby names you are considering, drawings, doodles, and any other expressions about your pregnancy and baby.

❖ Start a file on your computer desktop named "Birth Journal" and add to it when your thoughts get dreamy at work.

The most important thing is to set yourself up for success by having it in a place where it is easy for you to write. Don't invest this enterprise with standards or expectations that are too high. Let it be an outlet that you come to when you feel inspired to do so.

Approaching Writing: This is just for you. Your English teacher will not be scrutinizing this for form, content, style or spelling, so relax into it. Try to let it flow freely from your heart or thoughts with very little obstruction from your critical self. Here are some ways to break through writer's block in case you need to give yourself a little push.

❖ Write the date at the top of the page, look at your watch, and tell yourself to write continuously for five minutes without stopping. Focus your writing on your birthing experience with no other boundaries on where your writing goes. Release all critical expectations and simply regard this effort as a writing exercise (one which will no doubt catch some valuable insights and impressions in its net).

❖ Ask yourself the question, "What is the one thing from today that I would like to remember?" and completely describe just that.

❖ Write the one word or phase that most fully describes your given state at the moment, and list reasons for being in that state beneath it.

❖ Write a letter to yourself, relay all the news of the day and bring it to life since years from now memories will become fuzzy.

❖ Write your thoughts as a poem or as song lyrics.

❖ Transcribe a conversation you had with your mother, mate or friend about birthing or any of the sensations around it. Map out through your words how you came to certain epiphanies or conclusions.

❖ List the ingredients of your life as if on the side of a box of cereal or write a recipe of your days now complete with ingredients and instructions.

Extra Bonus Inspiration: I encourage you to free your natural voice in your writing. It doesn't have to be well written. It doesn't matter if it's impressive; it just needs to be true and from the heart. In looking back at my Birth Journals years later, what touches me most are specific descriptions of little moments, such as the nickname, *Sprout*, I called my babe when he was still inside me, or how it felt when my baby patted my back as I burped her. Be specific! It's the fine details that allow you to remember the real texture of times past. Use all your senses in your rambling account of this precious time. Describe the smoothness of your belly, the smell of your baby's head, the sound of his voice, or the taste of her kisses. This doesn't need to be candy-coated, let it all out, the good, the bad and the ugly. Mothering is all of this, deliciously so. I guarantee that the value of this Birth Journal will appreciate more than just about any investment known to humankind. Think of it as giving a remembrance of this precious time to yourself in the future. Preservation of memories is not the only motive here; writing is an endeavor through which thoughts gain solid form. To progress in your understanding of the world and your place in it, it's useful to have a record of the conclusions upon which you are building. Never doubt that this pregnancy and the first year are a rare opportunity in your life during which you are granted an entirely new perspective on nearly everything. Be warned; this exceptional vision doesn't always last! Reap the harvest of your immediate glory on the written page for snacking and feasting on in years to come.

Chapter Two
The Second Trimester

What to watch for on this leg of the journey

Balance Restored

The somewhat violent swings from ecstasy to exhaustion that characterize the first trimester have, by now, mostly found their balancing point. Your physical body is accepting this new passenger in your womb. You're settling in, like on the second day of a cross-country road-trip, still far from your final destination but firmly on your way. This releases your spirit to expand even farther and relax into the experience of pregnancy. As you start to feel the baby moving, it confirms your belief that this is, indeed, a baby growing in you.

Herein arises a desire to know your child, a kind of restlessness and impatience to know its personality and preferences, its inclinations and dreams.

Entering the Public Domain

The true middle-child of trimesters, this second one doesn't get much attention historically. It's by far the most uneventful one, though rich in its subtle pleasures. You are still too far away from delivery to begin earnestly dreading the pain or to get yourself too excited at the prospect of seeing your child delivered safely and in your arms. One perk this trimester brings is that you now officially look pregnant. Your figure justifies the clothes designed specifically for pregnancy with their empire waistlines and pleats just beneath the breasts that seems to send a signal out to the world that you are, indeed, with child. It is now common knowledge, public information. Your proportions are pleasing in this trimester and inspire endearing looks from many who pass.

Being cute has its up and downs. In a child-like way, it feels kind of good to get positive attention from ladies in the grocery store. In a more censoring way, you can begin to feel that the world expects a certain decorum or good behavior from you now that you are so obviously pregnant. You're expected to cross your legs, refrain from cussing, and keep your eyes a bit downcast. Of course, this isn't written down anywhere, but it seems to get communicated non-verbally, like a stern look from your father that perfectly communicates his expectations. You even get a little bit of reverence, like a walking incarnation of the Virgin Mary, an obvious irony given the nature of the act that got you pregnant in the first place. And you may be treated as though fragile, as if you are the vessel for society's collective idea of purity and goodness. Needless to say, at this stage, being in public can get exhausting. You begin to feel, like all public figures, approachable, and of common domain.

Be Fabulous

Regardless of its hidden costs, go ahead and bask in this attention paid out to you. Put on some sassy cat-eye sunglasses and walk down the street with pride. Admit you're irresistible. Graciously answer those borderline-too-intimate questions that will doubtlessly be coming your way. Let yourself get used to the attention; it will only increase with the arrival of a newborn, and you'll need the practice anyway. Let yourself swell like a helium balloon both in body and soul. Take up a little more psychic space than you once dared. Since you, as of yet, don't have a needful newborn taking up your quiet moments, feed your spirit with prayer or meditation or whatever it is you do to connect to the larger collective spirit. Send telepathic messages to your developing child within, or, perhaps, more effectively, sing a song for it to hear. Talk to it as you caresses it gently through you belly. Take long baths to regard your body and appreciate its new curves. Snap a few black and white photos of your beautiful new body. Have a last delicious fling with your mate where you get away for a weekend or light candles all around the bedroom. Celebrate yourself like a true connoisseur of a beautiful work of art.

One Traveler's Journal

August 3

Pregnancy sets the standard for how close I want to be to my child. Right now it feels wonderful to have my babe so safe inside of me—with me all the time. Yet there is a yearning to get to know this child, to see this child. To have perspective on this small individual necessarily implies distance between the observer and the observed. So to know my child I must be separate from my child.

This distance triggers worries and yearnings, but my rational mind knows that the natural course demands it. To begin creation of a child is to put yourself forever in a state of yearning, a vital state, a living state.

September 8

Strong assuring kicks from inside fleshy walls remind me of your inhabitancy. For so long, I can walk about in my life forgetting you are there. It seems too easy to take the miracle of you for granted. Perhaps it is because there's not enough to go on. You are all conjecture, my imagination trying to create an individual who is so hidden. The abstract idea of life is presenting itself to me just in the manner it always does (and this is why the rational mind misses it) from the inside out. It is not through my roving senses that I can know you, baby, but, rather, through tapping into the tingle that I know is your soul.

Though I cannot claim to know or understand you, baby, you are welcome. Your mystery expands my belly and my horizons.

October 3

I feel I've reached the equilibrium peak of pregnancy. I feel good now, hormones adjusted. I look pregnant rather than chubby, and, best yet, I get public recognition. I am past the likely miscarriage period, and the risks are lessened. The decline over the peak of this ever-growing mountain is just ahead. Then down towards the inevitable edge where beauty embraces excess, and the bizarreness of life and procreation makes for a kind of crazy energy that lurks behind the eyes of a truly pregnant woman. There's only one way out. Rev your engine, baby.

October 12

The waves of business from the outside world have been growing in size and strength. I look forward to a spring with minimal outside work and a new baby for Peter, JP and me to add to our insular world. So many distractions are getting like a crowbar between the complete intimacy between Peter and me. As I grow to know Peter better, since he is more his own person, somehow he seems farther away—the "benefit" of perspective? I must humble myself to the inevitable human cycle. I must keep a loose hold on that which I never could or would even want to own. But most importantly, I must drink deeply the sweetest nectar that is happening at this very moment.

October 27

A Get-Away Night for hubby and me:

Morning in a mountain cabin in Eldora, my love asleep, fire crackling, fresh out of the big claw-foot tub in the bathroom that hosts a view of the entire valley below, hair still dripping wet, face tightening because I have no lotion for it. It was beautiful to see the sun gush into the valley once it made it over the mountains and into my bathtub morning view. When I tire of writing this, I will wake my love and offer him coffee and warm bread.

Recently, while sitting in some office waiting, I read an article about teen mothers in a magazine like *People* or *Life*. One heavy-set white girl told the journalist that before the birth of her twins she remembered screaming in a panic over and over again, "Just get them out! JUST GET THEM OUT!!" I am beginning to feel a small slice of the claustrophobia I think she was feeling. When I can't get a full breath or get up as quickly as I would like or when I can't bear lying down because stomach acid is pushing its way up my throat, I feel like bolting. This pregnancy-induced claustrophobia comes on very incrementally. It's as if I start out in an empty elevator on the ground floor in a skyscraper. At each ascending floor only one or two people get on, resulting in me being pushed a little farther towards the back wall of the elevator. However, by the time I am nearing the top of the building I am squished and near-panicked, wanting to bust out and push down everyone in my way, clawing over their bodies to escape through that closing slit of a door.

Cathy has the both undesirable and admirable quality of being

21
~

able to follow her survival instincts with no time wasted on reason or etiquette. When Cathy and I were children, our mom gave us the honor of accompanying her to Washington, DC, where our older sister had just given birth. We were booked to take a small plane from Milwaukee to Chicago where we would transfer to a larger plane for the remaining journey. This first plane was small enough that there were only two seats together, an aisle, and then two more seats. Cathy, being the shaky one, sat with my mom and I sat next to a nice woman a few rows behind them.

Cathy started somewhat calmly. She sat in her light green, gingham dress like any other well behaved ten-year-old. Then the plane took off. She grew anxious. Mom tried feeding her spelling words to keep her mind off her worries.

"Receive."

"R-E-C . . . Mom, unzip my dress. It's too tight."

"Manner."

"M-A . . . I have to stand up."

"No, Cathy. Just try to relax. Sit down. It's okay. Episode."

"E- . . . P- . . . I have to get out of here!" and she lost it.

The next twenty-five minutes were hell for my mom. Cathy made impulsive attempts for the door, and mom tried to soothingly restrain her. Explosive yelps for release spurted out of Cathy that sent waves of unease throughout the entire cabin. I sat next to my stranger lady and tried to make it look like she was my mom to disassociate myself from my real mother and her exploding child. As the plane landed, all the other passengers let out a communal sigh of relief. Cathy tore off her seatbelt, stepped out, and puked all down the center aisle such that no one could depart the plane without sidestepping the chunks of Cathy's lunch. Maybe all our human-made methods of coping are cowardly and against nature. Maybe Cathy had the right idea. It is insane for humans to fly around at dangerous heights in a tin tube with stubby wings. Just as it is insane to idly stand by and watch something swell inside your body to the size of watermelon.

Cathy reacted directly to a perceived threat to her survival. With two and a half months left to this pregnancy, I'm not sure continuous screaming and puking in aisles is the best course of action. Maybe people learn to meditate just for trials such as this. Is it too late to start now? I want the results without the discipline. I want immediate release. Is that asking too much?

Yes?

Thought so.

November 4

The first snow of winter is my view outside our little house this morning. I cuddle on the couch with a blanket, wearing my wool hat hoping to feel warm. The sound of the furnace kicking in and heat blowing sends hope to my cold limbs. It is always at the first snow that I can't believe we go out in such a cold, wet mess. How can I bring a new baby into a world where there is slippery snow everywhere and stinging frosty air? Will this not offend a child so new and so accustomed to unconditional warmth?

The strength of movement from within is ever increasing. I feel what I think are toes pushing out way over to the side of my torso. A long child who won't take well to confining ways, I predict. This feels like a happy child, a satisfied child so far. It has not yet been introduced to hunger or cold. But also, it has not yet felt the strong hands of its father lifting it up to his chest, nor tasted sweet mother's milk. Nor has it smiled while its older brother, gentle Peter, blows in its face.

Looking out to the cold snow from my warm nest-house, hand resting on my belly, I feel incubated and incubator one.

Something To Do

Design Your Own Baby Shower

We women have evolved a rather timid ceremony for prepar-

ing our fellow females for motherhood; it's called a baby shower. By means of gift-giving, it takes care of some of the clothing and accessories a new mother is likely to need (and I, personally, have had some very tasty treats at such events), but it most often shies away from the genuine majesty of this next step in your life. With no malice intent, baby showers propagate a commercialism that belittles and makes "cute" the birthing experience. You, brave mother, are just the gal to usher in a more soul-nourishing tradition. As with any foray from the status quo, it takes a concerted effort and a bit of spirited courage to travel new and richer ground. If your family would write you off as a freak if you asked for a candle lit "wisdom blessing" instead of a baby shower with helium balloons, then start slowly. There are degrees of transformation, so pace yourself. It's a long road of familial and societal expectations ahead, mother, so consider now at what speed you wish to travel.

A Word About Ceremonies

Ceremonies are the vessel for the swelling feelings that surround life passages. They both contain and guide the outpouring of emotion and, through their structure, ensure that our intentions arrive at the desired destination. Practically, they give a beginning, substance, and an ending to a gathering of people wishing to honor an occurrence, a life passage, a person, a union, or a departure. These changes are not only witnessed by the surrounding community, but are supported both during the ritual and beyond. In nearly all cultures, ceremonies are not regarded as extraneous affairs; instead, they have an essential task that they are designed to accomplish. The actions are prescribed because the stakes are too high to be left to chance. In the case of the female initiation ceremonies carried out in many Sub-Saharan African nations, the practical task is to prepare young women for their roles as wives and mothers in their community. In this instance what is at stake is the very survival of their community, which depends upon the successful performance of these necessary female roles.

On Creating Ceremonies

Upon beginning, consider these questions: What do I want this birthing ceremony to accomplish and what benefit do I want to come of it? It could be that you want your ceremony to nurture your mothering community for the benefit of having a counsel of women with whom to share the challenge of raising this coming child. Do you want this ceremony to specifically welcome the new child? Do you as a new mother want guidance for being a parent? If you're already a mother, do you want to be celebrated and nurtured for the greater amount of strength you will need for the addition of another child? Do you want the blessings and prayers of your community? When stepping out into new ceremonial ground, it really helps to have a clear direction, both to guide the creation of the event and to ensure that you achieve your intention.

A ceremony needn't be old to be meaningful, but it does need to be well thought-out and beautiful in some way. Simplicity, elegance, and clarity are good goals. A ceremony can braid together various traditions, but try to keep one through-line that guides the gathering.

Getting Started: Talk with a good friend about the possibility of designing a birthing celebration that incorporates your values, personality and beliefs. Into this event, integrate elements that stir you most deeply. With this friend, discuss these questions:

- ❖ What do I wish to accomplish?
- ❖ What images come to mind most strongly around this goal?
- ❖ How could this association (the images and the accomplishment) be shared by a group of people?
- ❖ How could it be physically represented?
- ❖ How could it be spoken of?

Take notes and be very open and uncensoring of ideas at this point. This is the raw material from which you will shape your ceremony in the next step.

Designing Your Birth Ceremony: If you lead your guests into unfamiliar territory, they will want to feel as though they are in good hands. Give them the security of a clear structure, one that makes sense, and one that, through its design, conveys the purpose. Your design could be as simple as this three-part structure:

❖ The Beginning: a welcoming, to establish the purpose of the ceremony and give a brief explanation of how it will be done;

❖ The Middle: the substance, to do what you are actually going to do (keep it simple and focused), this is the longest part of your ceremony;

❖ The End: an acknowledgement of what just happened and what it means, a thanks to all involved, and a ceremonial sending off (or a sending over to the hors d'oeuvres and punch table!).

Some Examples and Ideas to Ignite your Imagination with Possibilities: I'll list some ideas that begin rather timidly, merely sending little shock-waves into Middle-America, then move into more progressive ideas, and finally into the grand prix, yeast-fest of an event! Find your place anywhere along the spectrum where you feel most comfortable. This ceremony could be a happy hybrid, one small step for Aunt Suzy, one giant step for womankind; or it could be a horse of an entirely different color. You decide.

❖ Into the structure of a baby shower, ask that a blank notebook (call it a Wisdom Book, perhaps) be passed around and ask each guest to contribute some wise words of encouragement.

❖ Ask all those coming to bring some canned goods to donate to a woman's shelter to acknowledge and honor all mothers. With the collected food in a wicker basket in the center of the gathering, ask all the women to hold hands and share a prayer for all mothers and children in the world

❖ Give each guest a tapered six-inch candle. After having your mother or some other older, trusted female light a strategically placed, stationary, bigger candle, ask each person to come and light her candle from the bigger flame, and speak a blessing over you and your babe as they do.

❖ With an empty flowerpot for each guest, scoop soil with your hands, plant seeds, bulbs or seedlings, and, as you pass the watering can, speak a blessing to begin the nurturing of this new life.

❖ Make your gathering beautiful and grant a feeling of community by having someone lead the group in song, better yet, a song that can be sung in rounds. Keep it simple and attainable so all can comfortably participate. Have a confident leader to coax even the shyest voices out in song.

❖ If you love the great outdoors and sitting around a campfire, consider locating a local farmhouse, campsite, wilderness area, or even a backyard with a fire pit, and light up a bonfire. Instruct guests to bring a blanket to wrap up in, and something they would like to throw into the bonfire (such as an old shirt, a poem, or a log). Seated together in the night air, ask each person to profess what warmth she promises this new child, and then, upon completion, add the burnable item each brought to the flames. Afterwards, you could roast weenies or marshmallows.

❖ Feeling homey and want to stay close to your nest? Make a triple batch of bread dough, pre-kneed it and let it rise before your guests come. Seated together around a table or big coffee table, ask each woman to sculpt, braid, or shape her piece of dough. Decorate your masterpieces with dried fruits and nuts. Once baked, each person in turn can tear off a small piece of her bread to feed to the mother-to-be, while professing her promise of nurturing for the new mom and her baby.

❖ If you love the wind, meet on a high plateau and spread quilts and blankets on the grass for all to seat themselves. Write blessings for mother and child on small pieces of paper that are then attached to the tail of a kite. Send it up into sky to deliver these loving intentions to the heavens.

❖ Integrate movement into your ceremony by inviting an experienced dancer, who is comfortable leading people in physical expression, to lead a circle dance with simple movements. Be sure to inspire your shy limbs with some beautiful music. Dim lighting, such as candlelight, does wonders for easing inhibitions.

❖ Some of you mermaid souls out there may want to have your gathering at a body of water, be it a lake, reservoir, ocean, river, or even a pool. Use floating candles or strings of flowers to welcome the participants. Then, wading up to your ankles or immersing yourselves fully in the water, ask each person to pour water into the hands or over the belly of the soon-to-be-mother.

Be Prepared, Since No Boy Scouts Are Likely to Be In Attendance: Anticipate what comfort issues, both physical and emotional, might need to be attended. For example, some people are extremely uncomfortable sitting on the ground, so throw some folding beach chairs into your trunk before heading out. If it's outside, bring extra blankets. You may want to give advance notice if participants are going to be asked to share words, since many people do not feel comfortable with extemporaneous speaking. Let people know what to expect in the invitation, and include a phone number they can call if they have questions or concerns. Clear communication is your best bet in ensuring all the important people in your life actually show up and participate. Ceremonies are carefully constructed events that are scripted and rehearsed by the key people. Do a practice run with any of the stuff you plan on using to work out the kinks. Discover the leaks, holes, and squeaks before the big day so that during the ceremony you are fully present and reaping the benefits of this bounty of love. Most of all, prepare yourself for the outpouring of love through this new and improved celebration of birth especially designed by and for you. Finally, congratulate yourself for clearing a path for all women who come after you, a path towards meaningful ceremonies that celebrate and acknowledge the unfathomable glory of birth and mothering.

Chapter Three
The Third Trimester

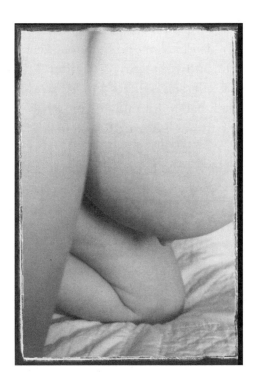

What to watch for

Leaving Cute Behind

As your belly continues to swell and the proportions extend beyond what appears to be comfortable or even advisable, you leave the cute phase. You may start to get a crazed, strong look behind your eyes, like a wild dog you don't pet for fear of it biting your hand. Knowing the job ahead, you take on the countenance more of a farm hand than

Madonna. This is the stage when the aches and discomfort enter from stage left and dominate the performance until the final bow. Heartburn entices that stomach acid up your throat, forcing you to eat smaller portions more often. Everyone seems to get their own version of recurring aches, maybe it's a twinge in your leg, or back aches from the weight of your enlarged breasts. This discomfort can arch over your experience of a day like an umbrella that keeps you from feeling the lovely warm sun, and your spirit can suffer. Take heart, Mother, enduring this, too, is a lesson with its ample rewards. Future challenges will most likely fail to intimidate you when you remember what you have gone through during this time, and what you've accomplished.

With just a month or two to go, you start to feel your body opening, as if your pelvic girdle is expanding with a relaxed sigh. You get a little softer, aided by the layer of comforting fat accumulating equally under your skin all over your body. A dreaminess descends that makes your view of daily-life tasks and chores a bit hazy and distant. Also, a peacefulness comes over you, an acceptance of the inevitability of life within you and its will to assert itself. You are flavored like a spill of starkly different spices with restlessness, patience, panic and hope, kind of a *Garam Masala* of emotional blends.

Claustrophobia from the inside out is upon you. As the baby gets more aggressive and antsy in its stretches, punches, and kicks, you start to feel as if you don't have enough rooms for your organs. Even your consciousness is invaded by constant thoughts about the baby. Hormonally, you can feel like an oversaturated sponge leaking all over your home and drenching anyone who should venture near you. Not only is sleep made more difficult, but wild dreams of birthing invade your mind, perhaps, preparing your soul for the shock of procreation it will soon experience.

Rev Your Engines

The final lap around the track has arrived. With renewed focus, you strap on your double D bra, try to squeeze your enormous belly behind the steering wheel, and prepare to floor it. With full knowledge of the pain ahead, you charge forward, even hoping to spur along the process towards going into labor. Furrowing your brow in worry you may wonder why you are rushing towards your own pain, but the part of you that can't bear the slow, dull, constant aches of the preceding months urges you forward. You scour your body for clues to your immanent labor. "Was that a contraction?" You are poised like an athlete ready to sprint at the sound of the starting gun.

Rare Vista

In spite of the blinding speed at which your consciousness may be rushing towards this birth, take some time to fully take in the view from this precipice you have reached. Note the perspective from this height. Feel the rush of wind on your face from this exhilarating perch. Remember how to see things with this exceptional new vision of yours. Make sure you have some memento of this time so you can remember it and use it as a frame of reference when life becomes ordinary again, just as it, thankfully or not, always does.

One Traveler's Journal

November 4

I feel myself opening much sooner than I remember with my birth-son, Ben, or with Peter. With still two and a half months to carry this child, I worry about gravity snatching it downward and me not being muscular enough to resist in full stride. The rosy side of this predicament may be an easier birth than Peter. When I pass by Boulder Community Hospital I feel the dread a mother bear would feel when passing through a section of the woods where once her leg was caught in a hunter's steel trap. Time should be like water, eroding away the sharp edges of memory, but it is too soon after. Memories of looking into the downward cavern of bestial pain with only one bottlenecked exit are still with me.

I recall when my niece, Michele, seven years younger than me, said to me of her childbirth in a cabin outside of Santa Fe, "People always said it hurts to have a baby, but it *really* hurts!"

November 10

Peter is off with Eliza and Juliana, and I am done planning my class. I start to write on some of my acting encyclopedia but decide to lie down on the couch instead. I just can't get enough room inside to even be comfortable lying down. No position I try gives sufficient room to lungs, stomach, and other needy organs. So I flop onto my back and watch you move. Your feet seem to like stretching to the right and your head seems to settle in on the left. Face up, your arms pummel out towards my navel. You seem to need a lot of room. I don't imagine you'll box yourself into a small, big-city apartment. You'll need plenty of open space and elbow room, I predict.

November 15

Last night, as I lay in bed in the darkness not yet asleep, I felt the presence of the unknowable collective spirit of life. Good Lord, is that you? At the same time I felt the movement, specific and deliberate, of the unknown child within me. It struck me how similar the two are in so many ways: profound purity of intention, elusive, self-contained in satisfaction, not needy in ways of human comfort to tarnish the heart's thoughts outwardly.

Last night I felt like a thin layer of humanity surrounding the infinite, while myself, surrounded by infinity, filled with air like a balloon in the night, hovered high in the sky.

December 18

Lying in the tub on an afternoon, cold sunny light coming in the windows onto the white tiles and the water green with bath salts, I felt like a frog that just inhaled a bellyful of water. I watched unidentifiable parts of my child shift and push out against the uterine wall. Then as I watched various sized domes rise and fall from my skin's surface, I clearly saw a head push up on one end and small pointy feet stretch out on the other far side. I saw how big my baby was and my imagination filled in a sketch of the rest of his/her body. With a swish of the fetus, my vision dispersed, but I saw you for an instant, baby. I did see you.

December 20

I am over-saturated like a sponge forced to hold more water than it can absorb. Hormones are all out of proportion, making me wish I could cry to release them out of my prison body. I feel stuck in my person. I feel really bad tonight. Maybe I'll trick JP into saying something to which I can take offense so I can cry.

December 22

This baby is twice as big as I suspected in the tub. The midwife assured me that this baby's head is securely locked between my hips. Thus, my vision in the tub was half-fold. It was the buttock I saw protruding and the long legs pushing the toes out the side.

I walk my walk and talk my talk and do my mundane, daily chores all with another human being's head wedged upside-down in my pelvis.

I am beginning to remember why the horror of childbirth can become desirable. The slow uneventful ache of so many crowded organs yearns for release. Pain is release. Pain becomes power for change.

There is a creeping invasion into my sleep that causes tossing and turning. I wake up while it is still dark and wish it would be morning. I breathe shallow unsatisfying breaths because my lungs can't expand all the way. I'm back on that elevator going to the top of this sky scraper and more and more people enter on every floor and crowd me back into the corner and poke and push and the door opens at every floor. I can't get a full breath. Shoved against the back wall, I can't get out and more people get on and we all keep going up and up and up . . .

Whoa. Relax.

December 23

Walking down to the Pearl Street mall to meet Lee, pushing the fur-lined buggy filled with a cozy Peter, I think about my dream from the night before. Having given birth in my dream, I had a chubby red-headed baby girl whom I loved so much right away. When I worried about it hurting for them to stitch up my episiotomy, I looked and saw that they had put my entire vagina on a platter so I wouldn't feel it. Boy, was I relieved that they were so thoughtful. Once genitally reassembled, I was being pushed around in a wheelchair by my friend, Tyler, when I accidentally fell out. After Tyler put me back in the chair and resumed pushing, I noticed I had lost my baby. We back-tracked through what was now a debris-filled corridor, and found the baby lying in an untidy mess, dust bunnies and splinters stuck to her crying mouth. I fussed over her as I gathered her back in my arms and wiped away the dirt. Well pleased with myself, I announced the baby was as good as new.

January 5

I am on the brink of something big. The anticipation is leading me to the precipice of an extraordinary view. Standing at the high edge of a huge deep canyon—clear sky with blinding sunlight, I am just about there.

I am at a rare stage that the world uniformly seems to regard as exceptional. I am overripe with life. I'm a fruit weighing down my branch so low that I can't help but catch the notice of all who pass. Inside I feel exceptional. I am amazed by my peaceful acceptance of my pelvis spreading like willow branches. Indeed, I am glad of it. It reassures me of the absurd likelihood that a nine-pound human can and will make it out from between my legs without ripping me to shreds.

Stomach acid erupts into my throat even when sitting up now. Even a belch is no longer a relief. This child seems to be long and very strong. It pushes its limbs far up into my ribs and stretches its pro-truding buttocks far out from my stomach, which causes the head to firmly press down on my tailbone. Shocking enough are its movements that I am, at times, forced to stop and curl my spine, hunched over waiting for release.

Later that same day

I have decided that it is easy to be nice if you feel good. Pain makes a bitch out of anybody. Chronic pain can really make you less fond of people and everything around you. Physical pain can twist your spirit.

That night

I'm leaving the cute and lovely phase of being pregnant. Terror isn't cute. Reminders of the incredible pain involved in pushing out a baby are coming to me in the form of this baby moving and pushing and readying itself for its mighty splurt into this world. Baby, I feel your strength. This is not the result of a faded memory returning. I know that you are uniquely strong with a mighty will. At times my breath is arrested and all activity must stop when you move.

January 6

What is it about us humans that we feel the need or see the worth in chronicling our lives? Why do we believe that our births, our deaths, our mating calls or dances, are of a different kind than any other human animal? Perhaps it is because we have let our thinking components become so expansive. We depend upon them so much that we are fully aware that we could think ourselves out of existence. Or, perhaps, we know that the unique quality of living we create can be carried on through us, just as the bulb of a tulip will divide, multiply, and create like flowers. How we live, the design of our living, does have an incredible impact on our lives and on the world at large. So if I can create some manifestation that evokes a positive way of living, or has a high regard for life, then it could regenerate and outlive my short spark in this dark world as a contribution towards the light.

January 7

You know how you crack an egg on the side of a bowl when cooking? When I walk I feel as though I have been cracked between the legs, and the yolk is suspended between my two cracked half shells, waiting to fall out. The impact of the crack resounds in my bones. Gravity is working on me, and that within me. Swollen, suspended life on the brink of discovering itself in the world . . .

January 14

The other night I bled two tiny dots of blood. That red signal released a torrent of dreams of my birthing, of multiple babies dropping from me as I swing from limb to limb in a tree. Gerbils procreating babies who are procreating babies who are procreating more fill the floor of my house until it is covered in a scurrying mass of fur. My water breaks over and over and over again splashing tidal waves of amniotic fluid against the Rocky Mountains visible from my front door. This baby is working its way through my pelvis via my dreams.

January 15

There is a lurking strength behind the eyes of a completely pregnant woman, the kind of look a strongman gets before he hoists his barbell of weights to his chest and then triumphantly over his head. There is something excessive, something of nature being obscene in a fully pregnant woman. The proportions swell beyond a balancing point. Seeing people look at me as I walk down the street, I think of how each one knows how this belly tumor got here and how it will splurt, mucused and slimy out from between my spread thighs as I scream my head off, I nearly blush. My dilemma is so public.

Conversely, there is an enviable acceptance in the soul of a fully pregnant woman. She is living a preview of her own death backwards, and she lives to tell about it, and (this is the amazing part) will often choose to do it again. The cycle of life has lifted her arched back high into the heavens and down around to be nearly crushed by the weight of the wheel. If she survives the experience and welcomes it into her thoughts and spirit, then a peacefulness is hers forever. Fear of living is never quite as frightening again.

January 16

In my quite disciplined existence, I have been able to force my will over my body's laziness and my mind's natural wanderings. However, my will is softening with my hipbones. I am dreamier, more meandering in my thoughts. I am very much inside myself. Outside deadlines don't seem so sharply daunting. I can work on my acting encyclopedia for a while (aided by cookies and coffee), but my attention won't rest in a stationary position for very long. It is not nervous or scattered, but slow and profoundly attentive to inward sensations.

I remember writing fervently years ago about all the disparate yearnings of my life, of ideas and desires shooting out in every direction. I wrote, "If I could just figure out what I want. If I could just jump in the air, high, very high, shake myself midair, and land soundly as just one person." Now, I feel planted and completely without question as to my place in this world. My task is one with our species' most prominent concern: perpetuation of creation. My discomfort and pain feel neither wasted nor meaningless. For once in my ambitious life, I can sit with myself motionless at peace.

January 18

A restlessness is upon me, like a craving for a cup of coffee after a meal. But nothing satisfies, nothing quenches the urge. This is a gargantuan urge to push a part of my very life out of me and assert it into the world—the bravest, most inevitable result of living. As I wait for this child to be born, or specifically, for labor to begin, time seems like it is being chewed by the most messy-mouthed child eating taffy, diluted by saliva and dripping sweetly from the mouth. Sometimes I catch myself plotting secretive ways to spur the process along, consulting second-hand wife's tales and rumors. Another side of me feels no rush and wishes to ride the current with my oars resting in the boat, feeling the gentle push of the river until it tosses me down the falls. Waiting for a moment that will change my world—the entire world—forever, such that no matter what happens, the deed can never be undone, the blood spilled forever, the first look, the first touch will always be the first, our circle enlarged and enriched in such unfathomable ways. I never thought I was patient, but I'm learning.

January 20

Four days till my due date and counting . . . I'm getting impatient. The pain under my right breast caused by the weight of the baby is like an angry beehive of nerves. It just feels raw and ornery. I try to position my arm and shoulder so the muscles are not disturbed.

I'm trying to move more, walk more, stand more, and then wonder why I'm rushing to my own guillotine when I remember the pain I am setting out to unleash. I feel like a kid at an amusement park throwing ball after ball at the dunk tank, but I'm the one who will be dropped into the freezing water.

Pain is release. Pain is something. Between inevitable pain and waiting, which would I really choose? Waiting is overtaking me. What to do with my hands?

> *Hail me, full of life.*
> *The Lord is in me.*
> *Blessed am I among women,*
> *and blessed is the fruit of my womb.*

January 22

Fear dissipates as I feel my body opening. Magic shifts and secret cranks are churning an open, wide passage way. Unseen gears and shanks are turning, only to be quickly and inconspicuously returned to their original shape after birth.

January 24

A most uneventful day in my pelvis for this to be my due date—I had so hoped to go into labor today since 24 is my favorite number and the midwife, Maggie, who delivered Peter, is on duty.

My thoughts are like so many wispy firecrackers shooting off in

so many directions that physical tasks are the only satisfying enterprise for now. Clean and clean some more.

🦎 🦎

Something To Do

Arrange for Your Meals When Baby Comes Home

This one is *not* optional. As someone who cares deeply for the
well-being of mothers, I need to insist that you ask a close friend or
family member to arrange for the first one or two weeks of meals after
the birth of your baby. It is such a small amount of work for the person who organizes it, and such a gargantuan help to the new family
unit. Besides, the people in your life will be thrilled to contribute in a
very real and practical way to your well-being at this exceptional time
in your life. People love feeling useful. Many people are hesitant to
visit when there's a new baby, fearing it an intrusion, so this serves as
an excellent opportunity for them to meet the baby and shower you
with congratulations. Never underestimate the soul-sustaining power
of food, especially when infused with love from your closest circle of
support. Also, you'll be amazed at your newfound appetite if you're
nursing. Word to the wise: call dibs on second helpings.

I personally have been on both the receiving and the giving end
of this tradition many times and can attest to its loveliness. When
receiving I was allowed intimate visits with my closest friends on a
manageable schedule, that being one a night. When preparing a meal
for someone else, I remember feeling honored and infused with purpose, as if I were an important contributor to this new family's nourishment and well-being, as, indeed, I was. Several times I have offered
to organize this for friends who were soon to give birth, and the entire
process was very little extra work, yet made me feel included in the
excitement of the birth. This tradition is one that tends to spread like
wildfire since it is so easy to arrange for and makes so much sense.

Think of it as a service to all other new moms in your near vicinity who will soon reap the benefits of your example, as you bask on this nourishing feast offered by those who love you most.

Getting Started: Ask a friend or family member if he or she would be willing to arrange for your meals. Give this person a list of about seven to fifteen names with phone numbers and/or email addresses of folks in your life who you think would be interested and able to bring a meal. Be very open-minded here and stretch out to your work place, your place of worship, groups you belong to, neighbors, and beyond. Include at the bottom of this list any dietary restrictions your family may have. If your home is at all difficult to find, write out clear directions for those delivering food. If you plan on having an extra person staying with you directly after the birth, indicate that as well so enough food is prepared for all.

Guidance for the Meal Organizer: Once you get the list, make initial contact with each person to find out her or his willingness and ability to make a meal. Tell them that you will contact them again, once the birth has occurred, to schedule a date for a night to cook. Once that baby is born, ask the new parents what night they would like the meals to start. Also ask them if they would like folks to plan on staying to eat with them or not. Then, get on the telephone or computer, and start scheduling. If you have more than 7 meals coming, it's good to leave a night open for leftovers at the end of each week.

What to cover with each person bringing a meal:

❖ Schedule what date and time the meal will be delivered (giving directions to the home if necessary).

❖ Mention any dietary restrictions the new family might have.

❖ Tell them how many people to cook for (mention here if they should plan on staying to dine with the new family or not).

❖ Ask to have meals brought in reusable plastic tubs or recyclable aluminum pans. If not that, ask each person to transfer the food into the new family's dishes and pots so the new mom isn't burdened with returning dishes. Another way this could be dealt with is to ask the person bringing the meal to drop by the home the next day to pick up pots and dishes that will be left on the front porch or doorway.

❖ Finally, ask the person bringing the meal to call the new family the day they are scheduled to bring it to tell them when they are coming.

All this helps to give the new family a schedule of who is coming when so they know what to expect. Now, sit back, and congratulate yourself for significantly contributing to the happiness and health of someone you love!

Chapter Four
The Over-due Contingency

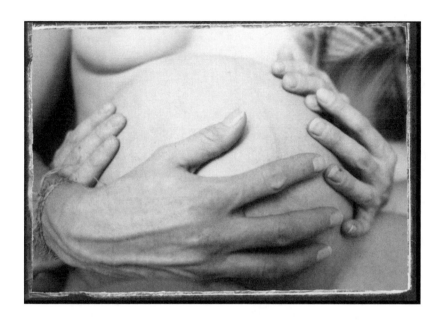

What to watch for

Enter Misery

As the poet Robert Hass once wrote, "There is no bottom to self-pity."
Nor, I would add, is there a limit to the misery an over-due woman
can feel. As apathy descends, withdrawal from society is nearly a
given. Any physical misery from the third trimester is now only
amplified. You may even be entering a state of disbelief in relief. There
is still a drizzle of hope and a damp excitement, but the waiting is getting hard to bear. It takes a disciplined spirit to keep from scattering

out of the moment into fear. As impatience with the natural timing of this pregnancy grows, you may even begin to seek to take fate into your own hands. "Relief, where are you?"

⁂

One Traveler's Journal

January 26

Two days overripe on the bough, and sick as a dog. Bad cough, lost my sparkle, gray clouds overhead. Ten o'clock and my baby boy is still asleep. He, too, is sick, so I hope labor passes me by today so I can be the one to comfort him. Disbelief in relief and slight sadness characterize these moments. Waiting and sickness are wearing away the elevation of my spirits.

Baby, maybe.

January 28

In a bad series of cosmic jokes, I have gotten a horrible, hacking cough that racks my body all the way to my crotch and leaves my throat raw and tickling. Aches and fatigue are the ugly friends of this jokester. I am miserable. I want relief at nearly any cost. Today I very much want to have this baby.

On Thursday I went in to see the midwife and upon doing a cervical exam she told me that the baby's head wasn't down far enough nor was I effaced. She tweaked at some membrane while her fingers were up me, which spurred a contraction. The memory of that crimson pain of childbirth gushed into my mind's eye like blinding sunlight. I dressed, left, got Peter in the car, drove down the road slamming the steering wheel with my fist alternatively yelling "Get out!" and then soothingly "It's okay, Peter," as his eyes watched me with worry. At the completion of my outburst, he said very somberly, "Don't, please."

That night I was very depressed. I focused only on the wall of pain before me. I felt like an animal trapped in a pit.

Friday was pretty miserable too. I was hopeful I would go into labor, but my cold and cough were so bad, it is just as well.

Today is Saturday and woke up felling very hopeful that I would cross over that mountain into the valley of relief. It is about 1:00 now so it is still possible. I took a poky solitary walk today and remembered what Mimi said about staying in the moment and not letting the mind skip ahead to more difficult stages. As I was crossing University Avenue in the slippery snow, a car turned quickly directly towards my path forcing me to run out of the way forwards. Like an over-inflated water balloon, I burst into tears in a shower of self-pity. The driver must have seen me in his rear-view mirror, because he backed up and jumped out his car apologizing profusely. I could barely acknowledge him, but buried my head in my coat and returned home.

I just sit in this chair in the sunroom, misery around me like a dark cloud. I don't answer the phone. I don't want to talk to anyone but JP, my Mom, or Juliana. I want release. I am hibernating in a cocoon lined in discomfort, fits of coughing, and a constantly running nose. I wait for contractions that don't come.

My thoughts run ahead of me like a stupid, yippy, small dog sniffing out the bloody painful bits. I, the disciplined mistress, must retract the leash and stay right where I am.

January 29

A malaise of apathy has descended upon me. A half-foot of snow has fallen. Peter has an ear infection that kept him and JP up until 4:00 A.M. The muscles wrapped around my rib cage are sore from being racked by coughing fits. A nasty little chunk of phlegm has nestled into my chest that will not let go for all the painful coughing I invest in the effort. And now I think, "wait, isn't it these same muscles that are so raw that I will have to use to push out the baby?" Oh, who even cares anymore? This misery? That misery? It's all the same to me. My taste buds for pain have been dulled. Just go ahead and chuck it at me, you ugly hag, Mother Nature. Same to you.

January 30

I don't even dream about having a baby anymore. I don't even think I'm pregnant in my dreams anymore. I am left unconvinced that I am having a baby. The sweetness of a young child in my arms seems so antithetical to this experience that I cannot believe it to be the result.

I feel like nature's cruelest joke waiting to happen. Occurrences in life may be random, but I have always believed the design of life to be with purpose. If that is the case, I rage at you, Creator. I have been made wretched and my spirit is twisted around my pain in an irreconcilable knot.

In a bath I poured hot water over my raw diaphragm muscle again and again as I watched a reflection of the sunlight off the water on the bathroom tiles.

Peter and JP have gone out. At 2: 30 P.M. I start pacing a figure eight around our living room into the dining area, circling behind the couch and around the dining room table. I play Schubert and then Bizet's *Carmen* at a near deafening level. I close all the shutters to all the tall windows in our living room. Our home, which is usually a warm hub of social visits and laughter, is closing down. I step hard with each step trying to dislodge the placenta's hold on the uterine wall. I look out a tunnel with darkness all around except for the relief of that one light for which I hope. I want to be alone. I want to do this work.

January 31

Woke up after sleeping with lungs full of phlegm that gurgled with every breath, to go get an ultrasound. The baby has a spine and brain, which is good. The lady claimed to see a nose and eyes, but I couldn't make it out.

Went to the health food store for cough herbs. While I was there I picked an herb book off the rack and looked up how to induce labor. I bought the Blue Cohosh drops that the book recommended and felt apprehensive about tilting fate to my desires, like she might retaliate somehow. Still, I took the herbal drops. Back to pacing the house and massaging my belly. I want this baby to come out.

Something To Do

In my experience, this time is so intensely monofocused on giving birth that I cannot in good conscience advise doing anything too heady or inspirational. Therefore, I recommend you pass the time by scouting out odd tasks that are likely to take ten minutes or less, such as cleaning the floor behind your dresser or scrubbing the grout around your bathtub. Think of jobs you most likely won't want to do with a baby, that a woman the shape of a walrus can actually accomplish. In other words, teetering on a high ladder to clean out the gutters is not recommended. Little nesting jobs such as arranging the soon-to-be new baby's drawers might be fun to pass the time. If you already have older kids, spend time reading them books to get them full of mommy-love before that new baby arrives. Scrub your frying pan with a wire brush or do your dishes by hand instead of putting them in the dishwasher. Mundane tasks can be a great comfort when anxiously waiting for something gargantuan to occur in your life, especially when the timing of that event is mostly out of your control. You can be a double winner when you release any frustrations or anxiety into these tasks that you'll feel good accomplishing.

Other than that, call a friend or nearby family member and ask her or him to take you on a brisk walk to get things churning. As much as you are able, get out, as it will be good for your morale and spirit. Beyond that, keep your focus on your strength instead of your fears, treat yourself well, and court the creative spirit with your prayers to bring you your baby soon.

Chapter Five
Birth

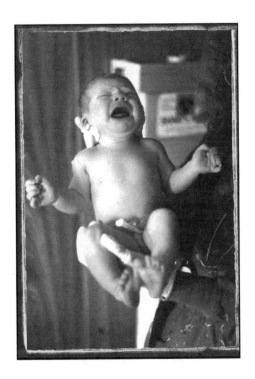

What to watch for

Forever Changed

Get ready to be metaphysically inverted, even though, of course, preparation for this is impossible. Here it is, the moment you've been waiting for, dreaming of, dreading, and idealizing. You're about to roll the dice and see what you win. Like any other gamble, no guarantee of how this will come out. Deep inside yourself you hold a small fear, but there's nowhere to go but forward. Irrational faith in a successful outcome will most likely dominate, along with the rational knowledge that, given all the risks, birth most often happens without a snag.

This is an exceptional time in which you will expose your raw self to the entire support team that you have gathered around you. These trusted people will see you teetering at your limits, and will be the ones to grab your hand to pull you back in. They will take orders, give you focus, and guide your strength. They will witness you birthing a part of yourself, a part of your mate, and the glory of creation all blended into one. Your mate will regard you with a new-found awe, probably mixed with profound relief at not being the one in the hot spot.

This child is a physical manifestation of your soul-connection with your mate that will forever be included in your most intimate circle. A part of both of you is about to be birthed . . . exposed, vulnerable, and free. The prospect of this can seem both ecstatic and maddening. You'll forever feel more deeply, have more to lose, and more reason to live.

One Traveler's Journal

February 1

At about 1:00 A.M. my persistent coughing leads to wetness between my legs. My water let go of its jealous hold around our child. Hazily I go back to sleep, little catnaps, chest loosening up, but still making me cough in response to the now loose tickle (God's mercy on a woman). Then I feel the misty, gray-blanketed hands of labor cover me from behind, moving from my lower back till their slow creeping arms cover all across my belly—a firm contracting grip that holds me for as long as it would take a galloping horse to pass by. The grip loosens and I lay back waiting for it to hold me again, which it does at intervals of about every five minutes.

At the start of each contraction, it is as though I hear the distant sound of the hooves running towards me, closer, closer until their trampling feet burst into me, wildly stomping through me, then retreating behind into the darkness. I must listen for them, because even if I am not ready they will still come, and if I am unprepared my first awareness is of a wild rearing horse in the darkness and myself underfoot.

I get up and call my sister-in-law, Jen, who has just been in bed a short while, and ask her to drive up to the house to be with Peter. I put our house lights on dimly, and turn on the leftover Christmas decorations outside: two red Chinese lanterns amid a spangle of Tivoli lights. They blow wildly in a magical Chinook wind. I curl up on the couch under a blanket and hope the contractions continue to build. In the still darkness I hear the milkman just outside our door delivering our milk. We are a kindred breed, delivering secrets in the night. After having called the midwife on duty at about 4:00 A.M., I awaken JP and tell him I'm in labor. The lights in the house are all on low. I feel calm and hesitantly excited. Groggily, JP makes himself a cup of coffee and the midwife calls back to tell me to go to the hospital. Jen arrives, sleepy-eyed and with wet hair, at 4:30. We get my pre-packed bag and head out. My amniotic fluid is leaking steadily, clear and slippery like a gel.

Walking out into the still dark morning, the wind tosses my long hair in all directions. The warmer climate blown in by this wind greets me and excites me, just as the warmth of spring does each year. We get into the car in the same manner we always do. We drive down Ninth Street just as we so often do, but this time nothing is ordinary. On the brink of a trice in a lifetime experience I see the entire world around me with heightened perception. I am hyper aware of the tires' contact on the road, and the bare tree branches fighting each other in the wind. Driving farther, I see the creek-side apartment in which Brad and Robin used to live. Both of them and their strange affair seem so poignant right now. Flashes of life . . .

The contractions continue. We park very close to the hospital and enter through the emergency room. Walking through the hall towards the elevator, I am struck by how beautiful the Colorado nature photographs are that are hanging on the walls. As I proceed deeper into this labyrinth of healing horrors, I sense something sharp and metallic about this and every hospital that dominates all the fake ferns and mauve carpets. You can almost hear the pain that has transgressed here rebounding off the walls, that can't be scrubbed clean for all the trying.

I want to get started, but I feel an impending dread. There is only one way out of the labor and delivery ward—with that baby pushed, cut, pulled, or chemically coerced out of my body. I am entering a black hole and can only exit out the other end bodily and metaphysically inverted.

They take off the clothes that I have worn almost every day for the last months of this pregnancy, one comfortable pair of black stretch pants, black cowboy boots, and my Dad's old plaid wool shirt. These articles fall to the ground like a snake's dry and useless molted skin. I get clothed in a hospital gown with an open back. I am clothed for bodily functions. The nurse starts entering the facts of this pregnancy into a computer monitor that is built into the back wall of the room. The lights are on low and the blue light from the screen illuminates the front of her. She is neither overly warm nor friendly. The sleepy midwife, Kat, arrives, and after checking my cervix says I am three centimeters dilated. The baby's heartbeat is low so she goes in again to push up any part of the umbilical cord that may have slipped between the head and the birth canal. There is a searing pain, but it boosts the heart rate on the baby and speeds up the labor.

JP and I take to walking the halls, the same path I walked, more encumbered with monitors, when I had Peter—even the same grossly enlarged pictures of pasty pastel babies. I need to stop and hold onto JP's arm when the contractions come. An older man walks by, and I feel slightly embarrassed. There are no babies in the nursery so we keep walking.

I like the comfort of lying in the bed back in the room, but I know that I should keep moving to speed things along. My irrational frightened voice beckons me to hide beneath the covers and let the coming pain pass me by. Teresa, the next midwife on duty, arrives also sleepy-eyed. I know her quite well from my pregnancy with Peter. The next nurse on duty is Kathy, and I like her right away. Heavyset, strong, and with a kind face, she is someone I can lean on, and, as an added bonus, she's had two kids herself. As any woman who's given birth in a hospital knows, your nurse is a very important person because she is the one who never leaves your side once you're far enough along.

A few months ago JP and I were at a modern dance concert and ran into an old friend of his, a former model who, JP told me, wore negligees out to nightclubs regularly, but is now a nurse. She told JP she worked in the labor and delivery ward of the hospital. When JP asked how she liked it, she responded that it was okay but that she was getting tired of listening to screaming women. My point? She is *not* the kind of nurse you want when in labor.

Teresa does a cervical check and says I am five centimeters dilated. I am feeling very good about how quickly things are progressing. Stronger and stronger, the contractions come, working their way up hill. As we wait all together we talk. Teresa is knitting a pair of socks out of fuzzy purple wool. I find this comforting. JP and I ride through contractions more or less just between ourselves. He reads my pain through the grip of my hand and through my face. The hill steepens. The knitting needles have to go down.

Teresa has me sit on the side of the bed and pull on the end of a wound-up sheet with JP pulling opposite. Giving some kind of resistance to the pain is empowering. It feels great to hold on to something as I navigate through each contraction. The back labor gets increasingly worse. I need to have someone push on my back through each contraction. I shout orders, "NO! LOWER. OPEN HANDS. YES, THERE. GOOD." JP's eyes hold me in place and keep me from scattering into the pain.

Encouraging words from him are like cool water on the hot pavement of my pain. In between each contraction there is an ease and light-heartedness in the room. Teresa has me move to a commode, no indignity too great when in labor, to get gravity to help things along. After a time, the nurse has me get on the bed in a curled up position. I like the way she thinks. The midwife thinks of the birth, and the nurse is thinking of the woman, soon to be mother. I welcome this respite of ease in my progression of mounting pain.

Throughout this time, there is a part of my awareness, the disengaged observer within me, who whispers secretively in my ear, "This isn't too bad. We've seen much worse, you and I." Just after the birth of my first child—my birth-son Ben—I hemorrhaged (maybe because the doctor gave me an episiotomy the size of the Grand Canyon and the baby slipped out too quickly) and the doctor had to internally massage my uterus to get it to contract, his fist inside of me past his wrist, so my sister tells me. Though in that moment of horror I had a lovely and ever-memorable vision of the Mother Mary, I wouldn't want to repeat that level of searing pain for any kind or denomination of spiritual enlightenment. And Peter was chemically induced making for artificial, relentless contractions, too cruel for any God to have designed. When having Peter, I remember repeating to JP in my delirium, "I want to die. Take me home . . . I want to die."

Back to this delivery, JP suggests holding one leg up while I am lying on my side on the bed, and this works. With more physical room for the baby's head to move into, things start moving. Asking for Staydol, I feel like an underage teenager ordering a vodka and tonic, knowing judgmental heads will turn. The midwife says that she suggests we use icepacks. I am firm and say I want drugs. This midwife, whom I know personally, has never had a baby and, therefore, doesn't actually know how it feels to push that last head-popping push that stretches the vagina to unbearable limits and often to ripping. With what I perceived to be hidden disappointment in her voice, she concedes to half a dose. I already have an IV in place on my right hand because of my history of hemorrhaging. Just after I watch the nurse inject the sweet needle into my plug, I turn my head and in that amount of time a numbing, wonderful, singleness of mind comes over me. I feel giddy with self-satisfaction but try to hide my high from the eyes of my midwife. In between contractions I can let go and relax. I focus in on JP's lead through my contractions with a concentration undivided.

Before I am at all prepared, Teresa suggests I start pushing. Now I remember, with my other two birth experiences, feeling the most unstoppable, physically profound urge to push when I was ready to push, and at this moment I don't feel that. Willing but unconvinced of my readiness, I hold onto my thighs and push. Ohhh, yes. It feels like an incredible relief, like I have just reclaimed the reigns on top a speeding horse. It hurts, but at least it is a different pain and one with seemingly more purpose and possibility for relief. I can't find my grounding while pushing. Everyone shouts suggestions of what I should hold onto or when I should push. Eager to please, I try to get a firm hold on some plan, but I feel scattered and floundering. I shut my eyes tightly while pushing. Someone yells out at the end of one pushing session that they saw hair. I imagined the baby still to be much further up the birth canal. This announcement gives strength to my determination. I yell out that I want to know how big the area of hair is because I had my eyes closed.

In the next mighty, life-determining, window-world-opening push, I make the determined effort to open my eyes. I see the head of my child-miracle come out from between my own legs. Wavy slippery golden hair swirls all over its head. The midwife tells me to make little pushes. I am so relieved, so anxious, so bewildered, I can barely focus to finish the task. With half-hearted pushing attempts, I watch the shoulders twist out and the whole body squirm into her hands. Teresa lifts the baby directly up to my belly with no detour. It seems an eternity until Teresa looks between the legs—a view JP and I cannot afford as our transfixed eyes remain stuck to the face—and announces it is a girl, the girl I want her to be. JP cries and I kiss him through an enormous smile. I don't cry, not just yet. The experience of childbirth, so foreign to the joy of receiving a child, has left me a bit too numb. Pain is selfish. Relieved, I gather our daughter up into my arms. I offer her the food of my mother heart and she latches on, her uncertain trusting eyes searching right through me.

And now the child is in the world, a feeling of longing and fulfillment as one.

Something To Do

Get the Word Out That You Need Some Recovery Time:

Birth Announcements for Phone and Door: Upon your triumphant return home, lovingly communicate to your world that you need some time to recover and to adjust to your new life. Beyond that, you need insular time to establish a close and trusting relationship with your baby, during which time he or she receives your near-undivided attention. Here's an example of a new outgoing message for your answering machine—soon to be overworked as you ignore calls to snuggle up for naps with your new baby.

> "We're not answering the phone much
> since the birth of (add descriptive
> superlative here)_____, who was
> born on_____. We need a few weeks
> of recovery before we can return all our
> calls or do too many visits, so thanks for
> your patience and your message."

You might also consider putting a note on the front door to remind visitors of your needs. Here's one example of how it might read.

> We are proud to announce
> the birth
> of_____ on

_____, weighing
in at ____pounds and
___ounces, and ____inch-
es long. Visits need to be
short to assure the health
and well being of mother
and child. Many Thanks!

An Entry for Your Birthing Journal: Since memories lose their vibran-
cy and attention to detail over time, write an account of the birth of
your baby as soon as you get the chance. Keep a notebook and pen
handy to write in when the mothering muse passes over you, which
will hopefully coincide with your baby's naptime. Include lots of
physical details, plenty of thoughts, accounts of sensations, and other
specifics that bring the event to life. You may think you'll always
remember this life-changing event with crystal clear vision, but the
passing of time plays tricks on us all, and confuses this birth with possible subsequent births. Write it down! This experience is a treasure
that, by owning it through your own words, makes you a richer
woman.

Chapter Six
Infanthood: 0-3 Months

What to watch for

Re-entry into Your Life

Coming back into the world after giving birth, expect to feel like an iron forger emerging from the furnace, a ferociously proud grin on your face, bearing your new creation for all to see, and to be greeted by the world with a pair of pink baby booties. The sad truth is that this world shies away from the majesty of early mothering. Birth has been made cute and soft, which it is, but it is also so much more. It seems more appropriate to treat a new mother as a rugged mountaineer who has just scaled the holy mountain of the gods, mingled among their splendor at that amazing height, and returned bearing a gift of unfathomable worth. Some may blame all this on society, for trying to downplay the enormous power women hold within them. I think it also speaks to our discomfort and timidity with broaching subjects that are so intimate and spiritual in nature. As you struggle to integrate this birthing experience and the subsequent amazement of having a newborn, you may feel that you lack the counsel of other women with small children who generally, in public, shy away from talking about the big things. Have courage and be brave. *Talk about it*. Be an ambassador for this stage of life and give generous testimony to the worth of this intimate time with life when it is so new and open. Chances are your courage will spark memories from others that they will be glad to share. Imagine a world in which everyone is aware of this clarity and love that is possible between a mother and child. Now there's a revolution!

Falling In Love

Don't worry if you feel a bit of a stranger to your new babe. Though you've been carrying this child within you for nine months, you've just met him or her. It's like carrying a sealed envelope in your purse as the anticipation grows, and having just gotten to open it and read the message inside. It takes time to absorb the meaning, time to interpret all the turns of phrase. Also, the pain and subsequent healing of birth can leave you a bit needy. Pain is selfish. The process of falling in love with your child has its own timetable and can't be sped along by "shoulds" or "oughts," so relax into the flow of your own speed. It may be a tidal wave of immediate adoration that rushes over you at the first sighting, or it may be a slow rising tide that sneaks up slowly until you suddenly find your self emerged in a swirling bath of love.

Guarding This Time

Cancel all appointments and cut the phone line. Limit visits to less than an hour. Have friends and family bring all your meals.

Position yourself in the comfiest spot in your home and commence baby-gazing and neck-kissing. To establish the bond that you will continue to build on for a lifetime, you need to lay a strong foundation. This is not a luxury for the privileged; it needs to be made a priority for every woman and must be supported by her community no matter how rich or poor. Other cultures understand the importance of this time and have customs built into their society that assure this essential bond will happen. In traditional Malaysian society, the woman stays indoors with her baby for forty days after she gives birth. During that time all her bodily needs are taken care of for her. In addition, she is rubbed with healing oils and massaged daily. She need only nurse her baby and tend to its needs. Neighboring women come and go bringing food, but only males from the immediate family are allowed to visit. At the end of forty days, the baby is brought out into the community for the first time and is given a ceremonial public bath, at which point the mother and her baby emerge back into the community well-rested and strong.

Conversely, we live in a society in which a woman is thrown out of the hospital one day after giving birth with significantly less blood in her veins than she had when she checked in, with a new baby nursing hourly on her engorged breasts, and is expected to land on her feet running. Rage against this! Right now, have the courage and intelligence to ask for and (this is the tricky part) *accept* favors from friends and family. This is a joyous event, and people like to be in close proximity to the excitement and to contribute to the family's well-being. When friends come over to meet the baby, let them make the tea. When co-workers offer to bring a meal, ask them "What night?" Have a family member come stay with you for a week to take care of you and entertain any older siblings. Since we're on a roll, let's pull the plug on competitive mothering in which new mothers brag about how soon after giving birth they were shopping in Target. This self-defeating, competitive model doesn't serve the needs of any mother. Since it is largely self-created by mothers, we're just the ones to deconstruct it. When standing up for yourself and your needs, don't think of yourself as a spoiled princess; rather, think of yourself as the brave soul liberating other mothers who will come after you from our society's expectations. When you take good care of yourself as a new mother, you automatically send a message out to the world that new mothers everywhere need and deserve care.

Girl talk with God

Being among the pantheon of creators, you may now feel a new solidarity with God, maybe even a bit chummy with the Almighty. Oddly enough, you may even gain a new sympathy mixed with empathy for God. In my experience, this direct-line access doesn't last forever so use it well. Build in time to hook in and be present. The position taken while sitting in a comfy spot with nursing babe in arms works well as a prayer stance, ritually calling you to prayer and triggering your deep connection. Remember that you get out of any relationship what you invest into it. Don't be intimidated by all these historically male-made images of God that sport long white beards or wrathful glares. If it feels right for you, visualize a pro-creative, feminine image of the creator, which feels as warm and familiar as your best girlfriend.

❧ ❧

One Traveler's Journal

February 7

The week following the birth of Melisande Lee was a very bad one—indeed, it was the most physically sick I've ever been. Still sick and coughing, I was sent home the day after giving birth with an over-the-counter cough expectorant and the box of tissues from my hospital room. My mom came to help out, which meant that I desperately wanted to be enjoying time with her, watching her coo over her thirty-fifth grandchild, and still give Peter all the love and attention he needed after two days without me. The truth was that I feigned good health for the first few days, getting up to make breakfasts, visiting with friends who came to meet the baby, and playing with Peter, until finally my body collapsed into a weeping heap in the bathroom. I called for JP through uncontrollable sobs, and he led me to the couch where I vowed to stay and rest until my strength returned. If I made a motion to go to the bathroom, Peter would become tense and beg me not to go in there, believing that room to be the cause of my breakdown. Melisande slept much, nursed a lot, and was gently rocked in her grandmother's arms for hours on end.

I finally made an appointment at the clinic and went in to get an antibiotic. I was diagnosed with bronchitis and given the desired prescription. Certain that things would get better, I picked up my speed, only because Peter's insecurity with his place in the family and his desire for me to mother him were increasing as the novelty of the event faded. Melisande also needed me much and nursed often in the night. Promising that I felt better and would be able to manage, JP and Peter drove my Mom to the airport for her to go home. While they were gone some gate to my flood of illness was lifted, perhaps because I couldn't bear to make my Mom see me suffer, and I went down into a shivering all-consuming state of misery. The pain in the muscles wrapping my ribs became unbearable when I coughed. I called my sister-in-law, Jen, crying. Without hesitation, she said she would pack a bag and drive up to stay with us for however long we needed.

A few hours later, as I lay in my dark room, unable to sleep, JP came in and asked if I wanted to go to the hospital. I said, yes, that I wanted to be able to be the mother of my family again and anew. A trip to the emergency room confirmed that I had pneumonia, and some serious horse-pill-sized antibiotics were prescribed. Lord have mercy on a woman and Western medicine be praised for what it actually can do; I was better within two days. A day after that my brother John (the one who adopted my birth son), visited with four of his seven kids, including Ben, who was then nine years old. They were on their way to Denver for his daughter's (my niece's) gymnastic meet, so they stopped in Boulder on the way to meet Miss Melisande for the very first time and visit for a few hours. After lunch and snacks the kids played, and we grown-ups talked at the dining room table. My eyes traveled from my new babe in my arms, to Peter, and then Ben, as those two sat on the couch watching a cartoon. I smiled, deeply satisfied with the gifts of my womb. "Not bad," I said to myself.

February 13

I look back on the week before this one, pondering the thoughts that passed through my mind that still nag to be understood. As I lay on the couch shivering with pneumonia, a newborn nearly drenched in breast milk just put into her bassinet next to me, I prayed to God, "Please, don't let her wake up right now. I need to sleep." A few moments later, her blankets rustled and she was crying for more. I felt mocked by God and bitter. Therefore, I concluded, God does not deliver us from human suffering. So, then, what can we expect from God? I thought of my Mom, who said that she never could have made it through Dad's sickness with cancer if it weren't for God. And, I wondered, what did God actually provide? Dad struggled with cancer for two years and then passed away. Even though I witnessed my Mom and Dad reach amazing heights of connection and love, still, he was not delivered from human suffering. Some people like my mother, seem to have an unquestioning assurance of God's presence. But not I . . . I am excluded by my questioning, and left wondering just what that unquestioning faith would feel like and how they maintain it in the face of disappointment. People use phrases like "God's will," leaving you forced to conclude that God doesn't really like you very much, or thought you needed to learn a painful lesson if you are suffering because God willed it. I'm not so sure God wills individual human suffering. I think we suffer because we are free and because we are alive. Being free, we are free to make our own bad choices and suffer the consequences. Being alive, we are subject to the design of life that inevitably includes decay and death.

Just days after Melisande was born, on a frozen, snowy day, I lay on the couch shivering with chills, racked by a cough and sick all over; I prayed, more desperate than self-conscious in the eyes of God, for wellness so I could take care of my own two children. Instead of healing deliverance, a ray of light came in from outdoors hitting a mirror ball suspended from our living room ceiling—a Christmas decoration that somehow had never got taken down, and the reflected light jeweled the walls with beautiful diamonds spread all over the room—useless miracles to feed hope. It seemed at the time to be a rather frivolous response to an urgent plea for help.

So then, if we can't expect deliverance from human suffering, what do we have. We have each other (no small thing), and we have these occasional miracles that feed hope that I think do come from God, miracles such as the heart-shaped rock found on the beach, the call from a loved one that comes just when your were thinking of him, the ray of light that shines into your despair. These miracles seem to me to be cosmic poetry. When I recognize a beautiful or profound or ironic connection made in poetry, I am immediately mindful of the poet having planted it there for my enrichment. Like poetry, miracles reek of intention, and since it seems they can't possibly be credited to any mortal intention, they, therefore, must be of God's doing. If I open myself to these miracles, I feel a strong presence of the divine Poet unable to resist adding a bit of encouragement where there is want. I especially like miracles because it feels a bit like God breaking its own rule not to interfere with human free will. With something of the spirit of a trickster, God seems to drop a miracle, tiptoe away from the scene, and peek from around the corner, hopeful that the subtlety of the lesson will not be missed. The nature of these secret God-droppings lurks somewhere between random and too coincidental to be likely. The recipient is left feeling that perhaps the divine does care, or that there is beauty in all things, that connections, perhaps, do allude to a larger meaning.

And do you know what? I am better now, and the people around me did offer so much help and support that hope was surely not in vain. Has my faith grown? I can barely get my head around such notions. Let it suffice to say that life is ever endearing itself to me.

February 14

I am shopping at one of those over-sized bargain-priced grocery stores with Melisande. Peter went to work with JP I have her strapped in the plastic safety seat courteously provided by the merchant. We walk the aisles, carefully comparing brands and prices, thinking forward to what I might want to cook in the next week. Canned music sprays down over the aisles like pesticides over a grape crop. I am glad to be in good enough health to be back to my former function in our family. I like being out in public among the living. Melisande fusses in the cart and I unstrap her. As though in slow motion, I lift her up and regard her just as some ridiculous 1970s love song comes on the sound system; the two occurrences collide like some overblown love scene in a helplessly corny movie, but finally I feel . . . I physically *feel* . . . in love with this baby, my daughter. My pain, my recovery, my needs had left me too numb or maybe incapable of feeling the love I knew in my head. I hold her to my chest, tiny her, and make my way down the rows of food hugging her fiercely with a foot ball field-sized smile and tears filling my eyes. That silly song seemed the sweetest melody for that swirling spot of time. It was as though we had irretractably hooked ourselves to each other's hearts.

March 1

Having just had a baby, I have some insight into why God may have divided itself into what we call creation. When the baby is inside the mother, there is a calm complete feeling, knowing the baby is safe within, one with you, perfectly surrounded. Yet there is an anxious dissatisfaction because this being, or potential for a being, is yet a stranger, unknowable. It is so close, so far within, that ironically you cannot know it. In birth, that vein popping, "Big Bang" process of separating baby from mother—God from itself—a wall is broken through; a single entity becomes two. Once the baby is out, there is the wild satisfaction of seeing her, holding her, sensually drinking in the child, knowing her for all her quirks, giggles, dents, and bruises. And there sets in a yearning for being closer than is possible, now that a distance between the two of you has granted you this perspective, this clear vision. This yearning kicks its heels deep into you and will stay with you always, making you feel that you can never hold your child closely enough, that you can never look at her face long enough, that you can never spend enough time with her even if you are together all day. This, I think, is love. Love seems to require separation or there can be no object and agent, two distinct beings.

And how did this entire cycle begin? I imagine that the creative force I call God, in a courageous and desperate act, threw itself into the wall of time so there could be a part of itself thrust forward that it did not completely know. It wanted perspective. It wanted to love. So in the darkness, we, that God-propulsion, see the light of like spirits in others from a distance, and we fall in love. We each kindle the God-spark within us, strengthening our own light through the instrument of our talents, so that when we return to God at the end of our time here on earth, God can welcome us in. We can regard each other knowingly, and, together, burn all the brighter.

Of course, in my experience, I have witnessed that all do not choose to travel towards the light, but rather, choose darkness in its many manifestations. This is a choice and, it would seem, a necessary part of the formula. God must have known that you can only come to know something if part of it is unknown: its choices. Perhaps God gave us freewill so it could come to know what another entity would do with the gift of creation. I imagine God also wanted to see itself through another's perspective. Maybe God just wanted to love.

I look to myself and question why I want to create children. Thinking about it, I realize that, most strongly, I want something to love. Also, I want the chance to witness what choices a child will make on its own. I want to watch and see what this child will create in its lifetime, given the tools of my love, my help, its talents, the knowledge of the time, and its own imagination. I want to see myself through my child's eyes. For any of this to be possible, I know my child must be free. I know I'm leaving myself open to feel sadness, to disagree with some of its choices, to even feel rejection at some time, but I still want my child to be free. For when the gift of love is freely offered to me from this child, whom I have trusted with all that I am, I know my heart will swell beyond capacity with joy. If I know all this about myself, then I deduct upwards that I know God. I, a leaf on God's tree, have God's design within me.

Therefore, I believe God is profoundly human and feels all the yearning of the heart we suffer, but six billion fold. Having shared the light of its soul with each being, God, I imagine, is wallowing in the most profound, wistful sadness teetering on ecstatic joy—the fluctuations of each human heart are felt as a parent would feel them, absorbed, taken in, caressed, walked the floor for, cried over. God is a yearning mother.

March 5

It is hard for a person so tainted and bruised, clumsy and imperfect to feel worthy of falling in love with a newborn. We adults with razor stubble, body odor, dry skin, bad breath, worse habits, suspicions, fears, doubts and dissatisfactions, are far from the perfect match for something as perfect as a newborn.

A surface perusal of a newborn might lead one to believe that it is a rather ornery small being curled into a ball (complete with legs that spring back to a folded position near the torso when pulled out), that poops yellow mustard, eats, searches for airborne nipples with closed eyes when not eating, cries and sleeps for about twenty-two hours a day. A closer examination reveals a smooth seed of the palest shade of green imaginable. There seems to be perfect peace between their sleeping eyes and their farthest memory. No regrets or doubts sweep their brows, just a raw seeking to trust. They startle when frightened and are instantly reassured by a touch. They seem to be searching for trustworthiness, the kind of devotion that will be there twenty-four hours a day, giving and giving and giving with no question of what is earned or reasonable.

But what I want to get back to is what it does to the inside of an adult to fall in love with a newborn. It stirs cobweb regions of the heart to watch a newborn sleep in your arms. When we look into their sleeping faces we can imagine a world without malice or forethought. With a newborn you can forgive yourself your worldly failures and feel accomplished just to be providing them a few moments, a time of perfect comfort.

March 8

I find it dismaying that women with small babies, women fresh from birth's oven, with strength in their limbs to grind timber to splinters, succumb in discussion to the most mundane aspects of the childed experience. To me it is paramount to dwelling at the edge of a flaming volcano and to speak of the rising price of grain, as it is to sit with a new life in your lap and limit a discussion to weight gain, diaper rash, and poop color (I take that last one back; poop color of infants actually is quite astonishing). It isn't that these, we, me, people are stupid or entirely lacking in awareness. It is just that the popular baby vocabulary is lethally limited. The accepted opening between unfamiliar mothers, "How old is your baby?" is annoyingly timid and silly, yet safe. I remember at McDonalds' plastic tube play paradise saying to an Asian mother, whose daughter was Eurasian, "what incredible eyes she has" (and they were, thin and long with dark, dark lashes), and the mother replying uncertainly, "How do you mean?" Protocol had been offended . . . unknown territory . . . invasion . . . protectors up.

Being a mother affords such delicious passages of time spent simply supervising children. For instance, I watch Peter closing his eyes, swinging on a tree swing, drinking in the dizzying effect of motion on his being. I help my friend's daughter, Eliza, build a sand castle on a shore that continually licks waves up upon it and watch her concerned brow furrow as she fortifies her walls. In a park now, I sit on a wooden bench as the wind blows my hair past these words. Children, like fall leaves, are swirling around me. This is a rich world for lyrical expression to flourish. Many of us have the time, if we take the invitation, to bear witness to the value of this part of life and, thereby, receive common words with which to describe this splendor. Here is a chance to perambulate around entire gardens with descriptions. There is no rush. This green open path beckons. My eyes are on the naked pulse of life as I, a voyeur, watch my children. And I, if attentive and a little brave, can tell the world of this precious, secret place.

March 16

So soon after the experience of being pregnant, and I feel such relief to be over that huge mountain and safe on the other side. I feel like offering my condolences to pregnant women I see now. In fact, they hurt my eyes. If one should offend my vision, I turn my head. Is that why our antecedent societies tucked them away from public view and into their homes? No doubt, a pregnant woman is a most disturbing sight. Like swollen walruses trying to traverse over land, they seem so out of place in my world. It's not prudishness that disturbs me. I fear not my child's question asking how that baby got there. It's just that I am as done with that whole pregnancy thing as *Vogue* is with last year's Armani. I shudder when I see one. It's too soon after my own pregnancy for me to be expected to be reasonable or maintain a distance between other's reality and my own. Survival makes us small and intolerant, driven by fear.

I know some people find pleasure in seeing a pregnant mother, thinking her to be so full of possibilities and the freshness of life, so life-affirming. Yet, still, I feel no envy. Life on a pedestal as a holy vessel, as the hallowed mother image, is a bit lifeless, ironically enough. No, now I have a newborn neck to nuzzle my lips into. Now I have a daughter suckling at my breast and looking up into my eyes, those eyes that follow my voice even when someone else is holding her. I have my prize and I'm holding on tightly.

March 17

Leaning over after a shower, blow-drying my up-side-down head of hair, I chance a view at my tummy. Oh Sharpei-breed, tummy of excessive skin. Oh, tummy stretched and emptied over and again, like a child's balloon empty after having been blown up by spitty lips too many times. This excess skin hasn't yet receded back to wherever it goes; it's saggy, relaxed, comfy skin, "make you feel at home" skin, "fits like an old shoe" skin. When I stand erect this aforementioned tummy falls into place convincingly well. In loving merriment I laugh at thee and with thee, oh friend, accommodating conspirator in warming three babes. Unmarred beauty holds no candle to actually having a good belly laugh with your belly, like sharing a cold beer with a friend on a hot afternoon.

The less than perfect secrets my body and I hide from the world through clothing are not shame; they're more like sweet old photographs of beloved people tucked in the bottom of a drawer. My breasts, slightly imploded, scarred by stretching to hold near-bursting quantities of milk, lower than they once were, get a friendly, loving boost from my favorite black push-up bra and the world's none the wiser. My thighs, now decorated with spider veins, get a slightly longer, flouncy skirt to dance around them. Out the door, that post-baby body—still cute for the wear and tear—pushing two babes in a carriage up hill and down.

March 18th

The patterned feelings that women experience before, during, and after giving birth seem to be dismissed by our world as being less than genuine because they are largely caused by hormones. They are given clinical terms such as post-partum depression, hormonal tides, and such. Yet I believe it is a fact that when I gather this girl into my arms to feed at my breast, that physical act brings on a rush of genuine love for her. There is the physical relief of my milk letting down, and they say a chemical is released into me that has a calming effect, like a sedative. Often this experience coincides with the fact that she has been crying and that I am calming her by giving her food and comfort. Perhaps just this, the combination of hormones, human contact, and messy bodily liquids, actually is love.

When my niece went through training to be a veterinary assistant, the teachers assured the class that animals, even dogs, don't "love" their owners. They have a pack-like attachment, and a dependency on the owner for food and protection, but aren't capable of love. That strikes me as a supremely arrogant thing for our species to claim. Believing we are the only animals that processes feelings and emotions as we go through these instinctual needs? Most of us have seen a housecat so carefully tending to her kittens, or been touched by the dog that gazes into our eyes with nothing short of adoration. Why is their expression of concern and loyalty different from our feeling of love? This isn't a dispute that can be proven on either side, but it does make evident a predominant human characteristic. We tend to desire to distinguish ourselves from animals and their earthy ways. We like to believe ourselves capable of higher things, like thought, reason, and, yes, love. We want to believe love is one of these higher human functions. I guess it doesn't matter if we humans have a corner on this market, what matters is that we regard feelings of love as genuine even though they are on the same tracks as our instinctual impulses and responses. Love is hard-wired into our being. By being human— making love, having offspring, feeding and protecting our offspring, the simulation of love is exercised. This is not an effort to reduce love to something base. Rather it is an effort to elevate the elegant and earthy path of love created for us and in us by Mother Nature.

I believe the rush of love I feel for my newborn when she begins to feed at my breast is very real. It is woven into the design of nature that she should be completely dependent on me for complete emotional and physical nourishment. Her needing me connects me to all of creation at the grassy green level, and I love her for that. I am an esteemed member of the creative movement that runs through the land, pushing up mountains and flowing through rivers.

March 19

Sneaking out of bed before even the smallest babe in the house wakes up. I sit in our sunny, windowed room and watch the sun rise in the east, coffee steaming, English muffin with jam in my hand, and I have the chance to write:

When I'm Not Holding Her

When I'm not holding her, my chest yearns for her small warm body to be leaning against mine. It's as though I've walked through my entire life incomplete, with a literal gaping hole in my chest that feels the howling winds of loneliness, but when I hold her to me, I am whole. When someone else is holding her, I feel myself grow impatient. I lean forward slightly, working up to an excuse for getting her back. But the real excuse, "I'm hungry for her," I never seem courageous enough to say. Instead, I say, "I think she's hungry," or "I'm going to check her diaper," as though I am too timid to refer to anything but the physical aspects of newborn rearing in public.

She is the most perfect expression of my body's yearnings. She is the spring of my disillusioned and cold winter. She is a cool rainstorm to my hot and weary soul. She is my faith that this world has a chance at not destructing by the foils of human hands. She is my belief that I am a strong and worthy tigress, lamb, and seahorse to ride her through her childhood and guide her through the brambles. She is my ancient mariner rousing me to continue the fiery hunt. Wonder ye then why I love her so?

March 28

If I still my body enough, I can absorb through my chest some of your peacefulness while you sleep leaning on me, little Melisande.

March 31

Babies, especially very young ones, don't have to earn their keep or say please because they are perfect in intention. They have no inner tally of debit or credit so they feel no inhibition in being completely demanding. They have no notion of earning care. If any one of us were handed a baby for an hour or two, even a day, a child who would not remember us and with whom we had no attachment, each of us would still lavish the same amount of care and attention on this child. We would feel compelled to do so because a new baby is perfect in intention. Perfect intentions are those not muddled by hidden agendas, ego, or memory of what is due or hope of what could be gained. They are perfectly in the moment. Thus, our reaction and response is likewise immediate, direct, and clear. The less perfect we become in our intentions, which nearly always coincides with our expanded abilities, the more we are expected to earn our keep.

April 3

I'm getting so much better at loving. I'm improving so much with this life that I lead as mother. I can be with Peter in his room after his nap and rebound whatever playful impulse he sends my way. I can watch him as he decides to turn his head one way, rub his eye, and then stretch, and see how wonderfully *him* he is. I can lie on the bed with Melisande and look at her with unpremeditated wonder. She wiggles and smiles a bursting, stretchy smile that wakes up her whole face. Then her lips reach to one side pulling her head along, and I know she wants to nurse.

I'm getting more patient with my ambitions that seem more and more like blind, driven beasts of their own volition. Life is getting more beautiful. I am clearing out the debris; the scattered remains of my former busy-work are withering and dying due to neglect. Good riddance. I'm not followed about by doubt so much—that unspecified, vague, nagging kind of doubt. I like being with the people of my life, Juliana, Jen and my immediate family. I feel wrapped in trust and possibilities by JP.

Life feels like an artful process, a three-dimensional masterpiece that speaks to my heart and sense of beauty. How my eye frames my surroundings is ever pleasing. Richness in such bounty is all around me. The funny thing is, that if I take an objective step back, I can clearly see that nothing has actually changed in my life for the better but my perspective.

April 9

I am getting so much better at taking in other people's pain. I always had the sympathy and love to give but there was an awkwardness between my intentions and my ability to reach towards someone else. I like getting older very much. I am so much more who I always wanted to be.

April 14

I feel Melisande's love upon me so strongly now. When I talk my nonsensical, rambling talk to her now she looks up at me with a swarmy, swimming look of pure love. She looks drunk upon me and I, in turn, am intoxicated by her, and so it goes, rebounding infinitely, escalating into the heavens.

April 18

Melisande's Voice:
Her deliberate efforts to speak her voice are coming forth more and more to an attentive listener who will encourage her on with a silly, sloppy voice. Her small new voice rides on shaky wings from deep down in her toes. She purses her lips while she goos and gaas in a mature conversational manner much beyond her two months of age.

She seems to be offering up her unprotected naked soul when she speaks, so trusting is she of the listener.

April 20

I must say I feel a much more comfortable, secure love for this second child I am raising. It is more for her and less about me proving my role as mother. I can really focus on her with a detached, wondering eye, an eye that has already witnessed the unfolding of one beautiful baby son and has an inkling as to the incredible worth of each moment in a child's life.

April 21

I'm really falling in love with my family. I love to watch just the small movements of their lives. I read Peter a book as he sits on my lap. Playfully, with a challenging gleam in his eye, he puts his foot on the book over the words I am reading. Instead of annoyance, I am struck by the beauty of his little foot, so perfect against the white page. Lifting Melisande out of her bassinet, still warm from a nap, I put my face in her neck and breathe in the peaceful mist hovering around her. I feel glad every single time I hear that distinctive Volkswagen motor from JP's Karman Ghia and know he's coming home to us. Down on my hands and knees doing my exercises in the morning, Peter gets beneath me pretending to be a baby buffalo nursing on its mother buffalo. Happiness is disrobing, leaving me vulnerable, with farther to fall. The only thing worse, I guess, is dwelling on the plains forever, afraid of heights and loss.

April 23

I want to keep this time in a bottle that I can hold up into the sunlight to be reminded of its color. Uncorking the bottle, I want to be able to take a long, refreshing drink of this sweet, carbonated time of pure connection. I want the feeling of this phase to be a smooth rock that I can keep in my pocket to reach in and remember the texture. Instead, I feel like a sieve through which my specific memories and impressions are already escaping. Like a fist trying to hold sand by clenching its fingers around it, the grains of experiences are slipping beyond my grasp. I guess that's why we chase our little ones through their childhoods with video cameras or snap photos—to capture moments that will remind us of that time gone by. Nostalgia is that bittersweet sentiment that casts clouds over even the clearest of days with our children.

Something To Do

Create a Prayerful Place for Yourself

Since you're still in a largely insular world, let this activity be a solitary one. Poised firmly within your mothering-enlightenment, now is the time to nurture a time of day and a place for your prayer. Devise some words or stance or action around the mothering experience for your prayer, something that seems fitting and genuine to you. Ritually coming to prayer in a certain place, at a certain time, and doing certain things, can trigger a deep connection through the repetition. It's as if you're training your consciousness and disciplining its focus. You may want to create a prayer unique to your mothering experience that is beyond your specific faith tradition. Nearly every major religion in this world was created by males so, naturally, few tend to deal with or draw from the mothering experience. By nature of becoming a mother, you have gained membership into the largest faith community known to humankind, that of mothers, who hold dear to their hearts core beliefs in the value of children. Celebrate and honor this connection in your prayer and draw solace and strength from this solidarity.

Find the Time: Think of it as part of a routine, like taking your morning vitamins or taking a shower. If you really asked yourself, you would most likely rank spiritual growth as high or higher than most other daily tasks, so plan your day accordingly. Make time for prayer. Pick a time that makes sense, one that works for you. If you check your emails daily at the computer in the morning, then assign five minutes before doing that task as your prayer time. If you have a quiet time mid-day when the baby is sleeping, then use a small portion of that time. It works best if you consistently touch into this prayer time at the same time each day, as it's more likely to become a habit that doesn't get missed. Try not to make prayer time feel like the unwanted child of priorities by saying you'll get to it while driving cross town through traffic for groceries. No, give it some prime-time attention. As with anything you create and nurture, you get out of it what you put in.

Find the Place: Investing a certain place as a prayerful place can be a delightful challenge and a satisfying accomplishment. It could be a place in your garden or by a window in your home. Make sure it is not a place where you are likely to be overly distracted, but, rather, a clear, comfortable, and conducive area for concentrating. Unplug phones and put the stew on simmer before you position yourself.

What to Do: Now that you're ready, what will you actually do as you pray and how will you focus this prayer on the mothering experience? As sensual beings, we tend to need some sensual experience around which to center our intentions for prayerfulness. Search for some element that stirs you deeply. What follows are merely ideas to guide you towards discovering your own connection.

❖ Touch: Have a string of glass or wooden beads and dedicate each one to some strength specific to mothering that you hope to engender within yourself through your prayer.

❖ Smell: Light a piece of incense in a small ceramic bowl and, with your hands, draw the smoke towards yourself as you repeat the prayer, "Purity of thought, word and action" over and again.

❖ Sight: Frame an image of a mother icon from any time in history and from any culture that inspires you. Meditate on that image while mindfully clearing your heart of any obstacles that keep you from being the kind of mother you want to be.

❖ Sound: From an Asian shop, buy a low and resonant gong or a resounding bowl that, when struck, creates a lingering tone upon which you can focus. Each time you strike the instrument repeat the name of a quality, such as grace or love, that you hope to disseminate out into the world though the act of mothering.

Be creative, open-minded, and a little brave in discovering what manner of prayer works best for you. After experimentation, settle in on some small ritual that works for you and keep it. As you continue to practice it, amaze yourself with the deeper and more immediate connection you have to your spirituality and the divine.

Chapter Seven
Age of Opening: 4-6 Months

What to watch for

Step Slowly from Your Cocoon for Two

Even though your child's wings are starting to spread out into such splendor, resist letting the gush of worldly details tear open your intimate cocoon just yet. Guard your time and hold busy-work at bay. Life is long, and there'll be plenty of time later to regrout the bathroom sink or respond to your three million backed up emails. This child still needs the uninterrupted glow of your presence, just as any flower needs clear skies to feel the sun's warmth. Clouds will no doubt hover, in the form of interruptions, dinner preparations, and bill paying, but do all you can to claim some prime-time chunks for the two of you. What is required here is your time. No substitutes will do. No financial gain for the sake of your family's well being will ever make up for or replace the gift of your time. Not only is this uninterrupted time what your baby needs, it's what you need, too, in order to learn all the lessons this life passage is teaching you. Be aware and witness all of this with open eyes, ears, and heart. This phase of mothering is a bit less showy than the ones directly preceding, so extra attention is required from you to glean all the wisdom offered. In this quiet time alone with your babe, you are nurturing the patience you will need when you find yourself at your sleep-deprived limits, seeking to integrate this new care giving into an already full life. Find the lightness necessary to keep a buoyant sense of humor as you get fumbled and frustrated. You are learning the endurance of mother love, an endurance more tested and tried, perhaps, than any other. You are entering into a place of real intimacy with your child, a destination not automatically given through motherhood, but, rather, one gained through the act of mothering. Surrender. Trust the perfect design of mothering set before you with all its pitfalls, perks and purifying fires. This is not a loss of self for the woman. This is the graduation into a divine knowledge specifically reserved for women who give birth.

Dive into the Deep-end of This Love

I beckon you to swim luxuriously in the sensual delight of this time as your baby opens up to you and begins responding to your love. Lap up those smiles and giggles as you dive kisses into the folds of his neck. Bathe in those rebounding looks of adoration as you two together marvel in each other's splendor. Everything's coming up roses and daffodils as your tiny little babe has made it to a slightly sturdier and more robust size, assuaging those irrational fears that make you interrupt your evening conversation to make sure your sleeping babe is still breathing. You trust your babe a little more that she can carry all your wild hopes and dreams for her future. Strange as it may seem, the two of you have had to learn to trust each other. Still, after all the times you responded in an instant to your babe's needs, and never left him in harm's way, you can see that he is searching for trustworthiness. You may feel yourself wanting to prove over and again, once and for all, your promise of love and care for this child of yours. His eyes may feel as though they penetrate all artifice as he regards you as his sole lifeline to survival. It is a gaze that intimidates, given the enormity of the responsibility, and engenders gargantuan pride, given the scope of the accomplishment.

One Traveler's Journal

May 7

Sometimes I am awed and nearly frightened with the power I possess as a parent. My children are so open to me that I can see the clear passage from their eyes to their souls and I, as their parent, can reach down into that dark young flesh and caress it or halt its growth with a squeeze. Every response I give, whether impatient, attentive, hurried, or kind, goes deeply into them. They haven't developed armor yet to shield away the coarser assaults of life. The responsibility of it is intimidating. It's as if they are the nub of a bulbed flower, and I am the gardener. They already have the design of their colorful splendor within them, and I tend to their growth with care, so their fragile pedals can bloom to full beauty.

May 8

To my children: Despite the obvious fragility of your humanity, I beckon your souls out into the world, my children, to roll in the valleys and to fall deeply in love, even to ride a motorcycle on the water front so you can feel a morning mist blasting into you through your clothing. In the face of the inevitable bruises and scars that result from living fully, know that there is a constant pillar of love from your home. I keep a living home for you in my heart that will outlast this brief light of mine on earth, just as I still feel the active, living love from my own father who died years ago.

May 12

During quiet moments with Melisande, I have uninterrupted time to attend to her splendor. I feel her drinking in my attention heartily and needfully as she nurses on my breast. There is such intensity in her quest to find trustworthiness. And I scramble in the wake of such perfect intention, humbled, dedicated to being that imperfect but unconditional source of love.

She wants so completely to feel safe—her startling, her oh- so-open eyes, her small hands, all her ways of grasping. When I can soothe her worries away and give her perfect comfort, I am rewarded with a feeling of peace and worthiness beyond description.

May 19

I am learning ever so slowly, as attentive a student as I may be, how to get down low and strip myself raw of my social conditioning. I am learning from my children to take no surface for granted but, rather, to feel it, smell it, and taste it. I am learning to roll with my children, to wear play clothes all day long in case a perfect climbing tree or a grassy hill should present itself. I am taking the time to press our bodies together, to kiss their bellies and amaze my spirit with how much love surges through me when I do. Our spirits and our bodies are tangled like a young girl's hair on a windy day. Love and its physical expression are two hungry replenishing beasts feeding on each other.

I have to learn to do this because we have such things in this world as thick clothing to dull the skin's touch, bassinets to keep her from my arms at night, bottles instead of breasts, holders instead of hands, daycare centers instead of homes. I am like a tail on their kite that darts in the wind through the sky. I can experience their freedom if I hold on tightly and let them lead.

May 20

Melisande is teething. In the middle of the night I awake to see that she is a frenzied gnarled wad of sucking and chewing. Her gums must be tingling like a barbed wire fence in her mouth. The bed sheets are gathered up by small arms that circularly feed that possessed mouth of hers. I witness this sight in an amazed but sleepy slump.

Peter wakes up and cries for the bottle of juice that he knows is not forthcoming. He's such a conscientious potty trainer that he wakes me up in the night when he has to pee so liquids are kept to a minimum at night. I go up the stairs to his bed, he is comforted not. I sing "This Ol' Man" and "Amazing Grace." As I go to leave, he pleads "One more song." I get downstairs and in bed. He cries again and I go upstairs. You know, I want my children to think of me as an ever-benevolent fountain of compassion and acceptance, but I am starting to feel more like an acid leak on hot tar. He cries again and I stomp upstairs. He wants me to cut a tag out of his pajama pants. He got me out of bed in the middle of the night to cut a tag out of his pants. Perhaps he doesn't have the breadth of experience necessary to know that that is an unreasonable request. I proceed to inform him of this reality with little effect. Finally I bring him down to our bed, which means I have a space the size of a 2 x 4 in which to sleep the remainder of the night. I wake up unrested, crabby, feeling like a hollow tree trunk, that may appear strong and steady, but is void of sap and structure.

May 20

Do we as parents reserve part of our love for our children, pending upon the reassurance they provide us by continuing to live? Each time I check her in the bassinet while she is sleeping to find her still alive, that beast of fear remains malnourished, until someday, I hope, it will die. No, never. Life does not offer such guarantees. Perhaps the best I can do is hope to housetrain the beast so I can bear living with it in my home.

June 3

There is a small window of opportunity during Melisande's crying bouts during which I can calm her if I get the pacifier in her mouth or my breast to tickle her upper lip just so. If my fingers fumble in the darkness, her crying motor revs and we are both on for another ride around her cycle of tears until the opportunity arises again. There is this instant when her mood teeters on a razor's edge and I can aggravate it by not delivering relief and comfort in time, or, thanks be to heaven, I can offer her mother's milk. She gulps it down, interrupted only by residual sobs, until her arm falls to the side heavily, and she is asleep.

During another person's times of sorrow or distress or pain, there are moments, instances when we as friends or wives or mothers can reach in that shutting door and offer comfort. We must be prepared, we must be attentive, and should our intentions fumble in the darkness, we must be forgiven as we forgive those who have fumbled against us.

June 5

I feel as though I want to pour myself into you. Not to make you think like me or approve of me but because I see the gift of myself so perfectly accepted by you. So that my gifts, my offerings of songs or praises or caresses can simply pay tribute to your time of clarity as a new one of our species here on earth.

June 6

A reflex develops for a very young child, about 4 months old. When I kiss here on her neck or by her ear, she turns her head seeking my lips with hers, resulting in kisses of unfathomable sensuality. Napping with a small child asleep on your chest gives a peacefulness rarely experienced in this life. Daily intertwining limbs, wrestling, laughing on the couch, tumbling contact is addictive! Why does no one speak of this? Why is that which is considered to be so pure—love of a child—taboo? It's as though "feeling" somehow carries a derogatory, soiled residue.

I remember before I had kids, hearing that nursing mothers enjoyed the sensation of breast-feeding, and I thought, "Gross! Getting turned on by your baby?" But now I know better. Just as my mouth can distinguish between ice cream and éclairs, my breasts can tell the difference between a lover's touch and a child suckling, but they all feel delicious. There is a difference between sexuality and sensuality, but they are close neighbors, which makes the sensations sometimes confusing to register. When nursing for the first time with Peter, I felt self-conscious and strange when I could feel my uterus contracting, down through the vaginal walls as he suckled, and the sensation was pleasurable. Later I learned it not only felt good, but had a utilitarian purpose as well. It was part of nature's way of restoring my womb after the birth process. It is within nature's design for us to receive pleasure from caring for our children, be it the calming hormones released while nursing, the protective pride a father feels holding his child in his arms, or the peace of sleeping with your child by your side.

We need to clean out our ears and speak purely from a loving heart about how wonderful the physical expression of love for children is. We need to shine that light brighter than our fear of its misuse. I know abuse happens. I also know physical affection is a basic human need, especially in early development. It is fundamentally linked to our development of trust in others. Those who do not abuse their children need to likewise trust their ability to give out healthy affection to their children and not taint the offering with fear of how it might be perceived by some suspicious observer. We know the difference. We know where the lines are and when they've been crossed. Let's not miss the feast life has laid out for us because of fear. It might just be that it is our trepidation, our censoring, our introduction of shame that is the root source for those desperate acts of abuse we so fear.

I want to hear more about the good stuff, more specific accounts of how people physically enjoy their children. Tell me about the time you spent a half an hour in the tub with your kids blowing bubbles as they tried to catch them. Tell me about the time you zipped your sleeping bags together on a camping trip and all slept together, watching the stars through the see-through mesh of the tent as you fell asleep. Tell me about how your baby son squeals with unabashed delight when you massage his legs with lotion on your hands. I want to talk about it, take it out into the light of day, out of secrecy, out of a place of fear or shame, and into an open field of creative expanse and joy.

June 23

Yesterday on a sunny morning, having a sixty-second birthday breakfast party for my friend Len Barron, he, Juliana, and I sat on her living room rug. I was holding Melisande close to me, donning her kisses while talking. My face brushed across the top of her head just as I inhaled and the overwhelming freshness of her scent intoxicated me. It smelled like a new idea before the obstacles are seen. It smelled like the inside of a bean sprout, the curly part of a sea horse's tail. I offered a sniff to those friends I sat with, and we all inhaled her with our eyes closed and satisfied smiles. "Undoubtedly," Len said, "my finest birthday present."

June 24

There is something damp and mossy about the inner neck fold of a baby. Wetness of shirt and mouth both reach towards each other to consume the baby's body. Where my baby's head rests in the crux of my bent arm, hers and my sweat mingle, creating wet, curled ringlets of hair on the back of her head and a salty flavor. The smells one can enjoy by burying one's nose in a neck like this are a luminous green, not for the squeamish, but full of mystery and richness. It is for those willing to walk barefooted in a dense, dark canopied forest. It is for those willing to venture into the back corners when rummaging through antique shops. I love that smell like I love an overcast spring rain.

June 25

I thought I was a more patient person. I really did expect that I would be a much more patient person. I could not have imagined that I would have annoyed feelings towards a baby who wakes up when I intended a moment for myself. I could not have imagined just how many orders a two-year-old can spout out rapid fire.

June 27

Though I get up to get him juice a hundred times or walk with him into the bathroom so he doesn't have to be alone at least five times a day, it is the one time I claim rest for myself that he notices. That is the endurance of love that I am learning. I have to offer a kind response and a feeling of safety every single time because I want my children to trust me, and I want them to believe they are worthy, interesting, and loved unconditionally and all the time. I know there's a difference between the ideal and the real, and that there is such a thing as spoiling a child. What I'm talking about is the human need for reassurance. I remember back to my childhood when my sister Cathy and I would call down to my mom every night and ask her to bring up a glass of water. We said the water from the upstairs bathroom tasted funny. Every night she would come up with the water. She had been doing this sort of thing for a long time. Cathy was her ninth child, and I was her tenth. Of course, what we really wanted was one more hug and the reassurance that she would bring the water, that our perceived needs were worthy. Looking back on it, I think she had the wisdom to know what it takes to effectively fill a child up with enough love to last through a lifetime. I remember an older male, poet friend saying to me once, "You think the whole world is your womb." I thought, yes, I do. I credit my mom with this feeling of belonging, because she set me up so well, filled me with such abundant love—enough for a lifetime. I recognize this and believe this, but when I'm dog-tired and he wants me to get up off the couch one more time, I am filled with self-righteous resistance. I can't help but marvel at my own mother and say, "Mom, you're a tough act to follow."

June 30

I'm finally feeling summer. It's absorbed down to the spongy part of my soles and down through my toes that wiggle in delight. Peter just needs the smallest jump-start to get his imagination running. He feeds apples to the crabby face in the tree to make it happy. We roasted marshmallows in a tiny fireplace we made of bricks together in the backyard. He loves ladybugs, sticks that transform into swords in his hand, grass that can be ripped from its roots and thrown into the air, and water—running water—the greatest joy of summer!

July 3

Peter's Assessment of Melisande's Development:
He watches as she wrestles with his now empty juice bottle. Through a Herculean effort and concentration surpassing that of an astronaut, she maneuvers the nipple into her mouth and sucks on the end ferociously. Watching this, I see him thinking. His brow holds a firm disapproval of her presumptuousness for changing beyond that which he had just come to tolerate. He is suspicious. Though the havoc wreaked by a little sister is beyond his realm of experience, he has a premonition of what this could all lead to, like aching knees before a storm. He thinks, "I'd better keep an eye on this one."

July 5

What happens when woken up too many times during the night:
I am on call at all hours, every hour of every day after day after day. I am a "first response" team of one. I have some two hour respites of writing time when JP or my sister-in-law, Jen, baby-sit, but otherwise, it's me. Contrary to complaining, I am just stating the condition of this time in my life. My children's well-being, contentment,

and feeling of security are my burning concern. This is my dedication, my worthy task, my good honest "tired" at the end of each day.

However, I get the illusory impression that after putting my children to bed, I am somehow off duty—that sleepiness will take over until the sun warms their little engines again. That sleeping illusion is shattered through a hazy awakening in the dark to a whiny crying from upstairs. Sometimes the complaint is a worthy need to pee. Sometimes it is a plea for more milk. Sometimes it is to blow a nose. Sometimes it is with no purpose but to secure some feeling of parental reassurance. When it starts to happen in quick succession with only 15 minutes respites—time enough to feel one leg sliding back into that warm pool of drowsiness—then I start turning in a "Doctor Jeckyll/ Mr. Hyde" sort of way. My teeth begin to tingle and I feel like biting human flesh. He wants me to sing "Twinkle Twinkle, Little Star" one more time? Through clenched teeth I manage to raise a rousing chorus of "How I wonder what you are," hair starting to grow on the back of my hands and neck. Hunch-backed, fangs barred, I clomp down the stairs back towards my bed, warring with my own transformation into a beast. I get between the sheets, tangled up in my own righteous claim for sleep and my desire to be an ever-loving and comforting mother.

We all expect perfection from our mothers, and ruthlessly remember any response to our obnoxiousness that is anything less than kind and benevolent. I fear for what sort of arsenal I am supplying for my children's memories. I want to be remembered kindly. I want my children to have a foundation of an ever-benevolent, even-tempered mother of infinite reserve. The truth is that I catch myself calculating when the first childhood memory occurs, three years, three and a half, four maybe, and pledge to clean up my act before that deadline strikes.

I'm not beating myself up about this all the time, and generally do feel like a pretty good parent, but I'm proud. I wanted to parent perfectly. When my kids let out an angry whine, I must wonder if it is my pride reacting in anger—angry that their unhappiness is pointing to some shortcoming, oversight, or lack of finesse in my parenting skills. I know these thoughts are extremely vain. These children are living their own full lives of which I am only one part. Not every turn in their emotions is rooted in me. Oh, I see! Humility is what is required here. No wonder I'm fighting this kicking and screaming. Of course, I know I'll lose, but that still doesn't untangle me from the trap of my own pride.

July 17

Though Peter is sometimes content to suck down a bottle of juice while leaning against my leg holding onto my skirt, Melisande squirms and grunts little dissatisfied eruptions of noise until I look at her. She wants eye contact, wants me to pour my moment into her, wants to hold me in her attention. She is a powerful seductress and can delight her captives with pure gurgles of delight and laughter.

July 20

It's just starting to sink in that I am, indeed, the housewife of my home. For years now I have been mopping, washing, and doing the dishes, but I somehow always felt like a fill-in, or a courteous house-guest who, humbly, without drawing undue attention to her gracious gesture, opted to do the dishes. Now I see that this is my job. In the unspoken evolution of my life together with JP, he has taken over supporting all of us, and I am privileged with being the prime caretaker of the two children that rolled out from the covers where we tumbled in an athletic show of passion.

Sometimes I feel like being a housewife is just my distraction between the times when I can write. But no, it is more than that. It is my meditation. It is the pasture upon which I sow my seeds. It is my chance to discover the sublime in the mundane. It is my test to see how many possibly frustrating situations, how many interrupted agendas, I can endure with grace. This life is the greatest teacher I have known, with lessons of patience and endurance, and rewards of sensual richness and lush intimacy. I am learning how to give with more giving as my happy reward.

July 21

Something has shifted. I'm no longer practicing or gaining training; I'm doing. I'm not taking classes anymore; now I'm teaching. Others older than me are no longer investing in my future. This is my time of giving. The transition occurred with no official notification, urged on by my own action of procreating, obtaining accreditation, and the natural progression of things. I mostly feel proud of this graduation, maybe a bit tenuous, but glad to pay out all that has been invested in me. Having always been the recipient of used furniture, just the other day I gave my niece, who moved into town, a dresser of ours for her apartment. It feels like I just put on my father's coat. I like the way it fits. I step up to his memory. Now it's my turn to give.

July 25

Further thoughts on my place in the world:

I have always felt spiritually immature when I look at Buddhism. I just can't get my head around the whole notion of meditation and gaining a state of "no mind." It seems by doing that, I'd be practicing being dead. I'll have plenty of time to meditate and enter a state of "no mind" when I'm dead and truly have no mind. While I'm alive, I just want to do the living part, the doing, and the creating. I don't mind the futility of it. I see that it's futile. I've noticed. That really doesn't bother me because the doing of it feels good enough and is ample reward in itself. It seems like I only ever get a higher level of consciousness through lessons learned while I am *doing* something (usually the wrong way). I've heard the benefits of meditation exalted by many sources, of how it can be a source of grounding for all else that you do. I think I have Attention Deficit Disorder of the soul. My desires are a runaway cart on the hill of life. I've too uncontrollable a hunger for life to stop gorging on the feast. Sitting still for any length of time is beyond me. I worry that if I stop *doing* before my time—into a stagnant pool of contemplation and meditation—there might just not be enough there to work with. When we near death, I imagine we begin to naturally take on the pure being, like switching from a small, outgrown coat to a larger, more comfortable one. Perhaps maturity is knowing when the *doing* is done and the being begins.

July 29

There was a hot summer day. A baby girl just a half a year in this world was in her Mama's arms. I, the mama, felt her warm skin on mine. Then on the back of her neck I discovered several cucumber seeds from a piece of cucumber she managed to place in her mouth earlier on. My lips kissed those juicy bits off her smooth skin. I chopped those seeds with my front teeth and swallowed them with a smiling mouth and closed eyes.

Something To Do

Celebrate Your Shared Sensuality with Baby

Discovering ways to be physically close and playful with your baby is both the challenge and the payoff for this phase of your journey. The creation of this exchange is something that can be led by you, yet prompted by your baby. Repetition is highly encouraged, as it will only increase the delight your child experiences in these interactions together. Through your physical gift of love outpoured, your baby will learn intimacy and have her capacity for intimacy expanded. Lucky you, mother, for you will be the primary benefactor of this investment!

Getting Started: It is far too easy to skim through a day without ever making a deep and real contact with your baby. It seems to take a concerted effort to allot time for just the two of you to swim in each other's eyes, dive into each other's touch, and belly flop into shared laughs. You may feel shy introducing new ideas of intimacy for you and your baby to share, but go ahead. Start slowly, but keep going! Here are some ideas that might suit you.

❖ As much as your back can take it, carry your baby in a front pack, baby sling, or backpack so that your baby can hear your voice, feel your body, and move in perfect synchronization to the rhythm of your movements.

❖ Play silly games with your baby straddling your legs as you sit holding his hands. Lift one knee and then the other as your baby wobbles back and forth gently, saying "Farmer goes a trotting, a trotting, a trotting, Farmer goes a trotting to market one day." Speed up your knees as you say, "Lady goes a cantering, a cantering, a cantering, Lady goes a cantering to market one day." Let both legs bounce baby in increasing energy as you say "Gentleman goes a galloping, a galloping, a galloping. Gentleman goes a galloping to market one day."

❖ Go swimming together with baby in your arms and enjoy the physical togetherness this recreation naturally brings with it. See how many ways you can suspend and support her in the water.

❖ *Play peek-a-boo by putting a cloth over baby's head, asking "Where's my baby?" Pull the cloth off and exclaim with nothing short of elation, "There you are!"

Upping the Ante: Go on, throw another quarter in the kitty and up the stakes. Let's move on to some less traveled, yet, naturally, slightly more exciting forays into mother and baby intimacy.

❖ Buy some body crayons and draw beautiful designs on you and babe in the bath. Let him nurse on your breast and delight in the visual beauty of the butterfly drawn on your chest all at once.

❖ Turn on your favorite slow dance song, turn the lights down low and dance together cheek to cheek, of course, singing along at top volume. Don't forget the dips and stolen kisses.

❖ Go outside and both lay down with your tummies to the grass face to face. Delight in touching the blades of grass and the feeling of the warm sun on your backs. Double your fun by throwing a blanket over the two of you and begin rolling as a mass of baby, mom, and blanket.

❖ Have a staring contest with your baby where you stare into her eyes and try to make her laugh before she cracks you up into giggles. As a friendly warning, be prepared to lose. Stare longer than you ever have before into her eyes and see where it takes you both.

❖ On a warm rainy day, get your bathing suit on, strip your baby and head out into the rain together fully surrendering to getting wet.

Even tip your heads back with open mouths and try to catch the drops mid-flight.

No doubt you and your baby already have many ways of being close. Nurture these, expand upon them and never doubt their worth. Your baby needs your lead in celebrating sensuality. Ask your parents what physical games they played with you. Get some oldies but good-ies from the grandparents. Ask your friends what they like to do to be intimate with their babies. Share ideas just as you would share a favorite recipe. Trust the goodness of physically expressing love to our children. Then, let the feast of togetherness begin!

Chapter Eight
Age of Discovery: 7-9 Months

What to watch for

Premonitions of the Separation to Come

Ah, life is beginning to wedge its way into that perfect connection you have with your babe. Presenting itself in myriad forms, life pries you away from each other by returning your ambition to you such that you feel a restlessness and an urge to get out on your own. It comes over you like sobriety after a night of Dionysian revels. Now that the preverbal party's nearly over, the needs of your child may begin to feel like a weight pinning you down and taking all your time. You might even be feeling an inkling of desire to get pregnant with a next child, which would definitely prove to be a very physical, belly-sized wedge between you and your little one. On your baby's side, life, in the form of curiosity, entices her out of your mommy-orbit to travel further from your body than ever before, and the lure of independence fills her with impudence and pride. She can sit by herself ever so confidently and, most likely, even crawl away with hardly a look back. Not only that, but nutritionists suggest that your child now gain nourishment from sources other than your own body's providing. The traitor! She's now snacking on Cheerios and strained plums with no regard whatsoever for your delicate self-esteem. These small steps towards separation can strike fear in the heart of both mother and child, resulting in ferocious hugs and half-hour nursing sessions to ward off the inevitable. Up until now, it's as if you've both fooled yourselves into thinking you are still one, and neither of you is yet willing to consider the evidence stacked up against that comforting belief.

Grace Descending

However, there are gifts that come with this acceptance of you two as separate beings. Just as you can feel in your own life the separateness yet union with the divine, you will teeter between these same feelings with your child. As you learn to trust your connection with your child, even though you are not as body-linked anymore, so too you may grow into a more trusting relationship with the divine and its sometimes illusive presence in your life. Likewise, the humility found in putting your child's needs above your own immediate desires again and again engenders a very mature form of acceptance. You have recognized your role in our most fundamental drive as a people—to perpetuate the species, that God-designed core of our existence. You may feel consumed by God's will, but in a good way, as if you are a part of it and not separate from it. It's as though you are complicit and not raging for your own free will, a form of submission that does not result in loss. It may feel like a shower of light-as-air feathers comforting and surrounding you, filling your view with nothing but the grace and love of God.

Also, maturity in all its best manifestations comes upon you. You can most likely begin to feel age descending, but it is comfortable and has its own beauty. Another awareness that arises is of the power of the repeated rituals of nurturing, and other tasks that you repeat many times a day, day after day after day. Mid-task you may find yourself overwhelmed by the beauty of these gestures. Awe, in the form of reverence and wonder, is inspired in you daily as you flower into a more perceptive you. The clarity and perfection of your babe's expressions, the marvel of him discovering how to manipulate his environment, and the opportunity to be the lucky one witnessing all of this, is a prize for which you are most grateful. Gratitude, ah, gratitude—one of the most pleasing qualities to feel and dwell within. You've got gratitude in spades.

One Traveler's Journal

August 9

Melisande has begun solid foods—mashed apples and flaky baby rice cereal—and thus her poop has changed. She now has regular, icky-smelling poop, whereas before she had sweet-smelling, turmeric-yellow-mustard poop, the kind a baby who is only nursing has. This change may seem an odd thing to note, but it is significant, indeed. That saturated, sweet smell of baby poop enters a parent's heart like humidity into the woodwork of an old house. The loss of that surprisingly pleasant scent alerts parents that their baby is growing up. The parent must mourn the loss of infanthood as he or she celebrates the gaining independence that will someday make this baby want to fly away to feel the wind beneath its wings. I tell other parents of this development and they give me a warm consolatory smile, knowing the bittersweet nature of this time of moving on.

August 17

Melisande is propelled forward, upward, and onward in her development by dissatisfaction. She watches her hand try to pick up a crumbled piece of paper off the floor, but is unable to position her hand effectively before the fingers bend in. She frowns at her hand. There is nothing cute about this determination. Surely babies do not desire dopey clown faces on their practice material. If you put a TV remote control or some goofy toy in front of a baby, she will certainly reach for the black tool with fascinating buttons and some unknown purpose. There's nothing cute about such strong intensity.

August 18

I sleep with her every night. She lies on her side facing me, her head resting on my arm, as I lie on my side with my other arm over her, hugging her close to me. In the dark of night she rustles about, awakened by a hungry feeling in her hollow stomach. I wake up and look at her by the light that steals into our bedroom. I can see her big eyes searching for mine. She finds them in just barely enough light and is reassured. I unbutton my nightgown and she latches on to my breast almost asleep already, knowing the warm satisfaction of mother's milk is forthcoming and riding down her throat. Another four hours pass in a world of dreams and suspended existence until we repeat this ritual, only that I roll her onto my belly and plop her down on the other side of my body to nurse on the other breast. There is a religious quality to repeating these patterns again and again, sometimes drowsy, sometimes mindful, sometimes bored, sometimes aware.

August 20

After having Peter, my former physical state returned, slightly altered, after about eight months. Now I have had two children. My youngest is still less than one year old. The combination of compromised sleep, nursing, outside obligations, household chores, and the task of watching after two children is taking its toll on my appearance. I feel a heavy tiredness in my face that pulls at my hollowed checks. There is a roughness, a wild tiredness, a panting-dog-look in my eyes. My body is not tight and firm in all the right places. I am strong like a farmhand, not like someone who attentively tones her body. I have tanned shoulders from where my tank top stops, no bikini lines for this mother who has resorted to wearing a one piece with a wrap skirt.

I sense that when this littlest one can walk and I stop nursing, much of my former energy and shape will return. I am not so heartily mourning the loss of my figure that once bopped topless in the Greek islands, for she was a yearning silly girl in many ways. It is simply interesting to note that women get a taste of being desirable and beautiful as young women when every girl, flushed with the excitement and possibility of youth, is irresistible. As we bear children and become strengthened for the labor of daily living, we women gain a rugged appeal that is beautiful as wild grass and warm as a wool blanket. With the passing years, some mothers choose not to gracefully wrap this new shawl of beauty around them, but instead, become tempted to re-dip their finger into that sweet honey pot of youth. They mistakenly think that now that there are no toddlers swinging from their apron strings, with proper preening they can be flouncy young girls again. The results of such efforts are almost always a little sad. Good honest aging is beautiful only when embraced, and is garish when painted over with a pastel attempt to pretend that sorrows and joys haven't had their way with you and left their tracks.

The face is a masterpiece that takes a lifetime to complete. It is each person's autobiography, each person's road map to the paths her life has taken. Each face is unique to the world as a thumbprint. An old face is much more its own than a young face that has yet to grow into itself. Aging, take my arm and lead me to your comfort. I'll try not to protest nor drag my feet.

August 23

Melisande is sitting in her wooden highchair looking about as small as any sitting human could. It's a hot day so she is wearing only her diaper. I have put some dry crispy rice cereal in front of her and she is quite seriously pursuing the pieces. Selecting one, she then tries to maneuver it into her mouth. She has the tiny crispies adhered to unimaginable places all over her body. She surveys the tray that is just inches beneath her chin with the authority of an inspector, considers the amount of effort exerted to successfully land a piece of the cereal into her mouth, balanced with the actual size of the pieces, and resigns herself to chewing on a little doll instead.

September 2

When she startles awake, she opens her awareness and simultaneously begins her visual search for my face. Upon seeing my ready expression, raw fear falls from her like old shingles from a roof. She is raging against the separating of our selves. We console each other against the inevitable by sleeping together, by me holding her most of the day while I do other things. The fact that I can unconsciously do so many things with her on my lap, hip, or in some on-body contraption attests to our oneness. For if I were directing my attention towards her during those times, that would actually expose our separateness as one being looking at an independent other. Otherness is what she fears and for good reason. I am her meal, her rest and shelter, her protector. I am her human touch, her fountain, her home.

September 3

I have many rational reasons for not wanting to become pregnant again. In discussions, JP and I have deemed overpopulation to be one of the leading causes of stress on our world today and have stated we only wanted to have two children biologically. We don't have room in our small, somewhat funky old house for more kids. We can't afford another birth. I told my body this was the last I'd ever make it endure.

Yet and still . . . as I in my private moment feel down towards my belly with my hand, I thrill at the possibility of life. I have not gotten my period back yet. Yes, I am still nursing, but still and yet . . . .. Yes, JP has had a vasectomy, but we did have unprotected and surely life-enticing lovemaking before the supposed "safe" period of waiting (both of us wistfully tempting the finality of our decision, beckoning one last child to slip though the improbability into our lives).

I suspect there is a part of every person who has ever dipped a foot in the immortalizing stream of reproduction that is ever-ready to do it again and again and again. At the possibility of being pregnant, I hear from this part of me a clear and resolute "yes." This is the part of me that is separate from my societal context of intellectual, existentialist, and psychological inquiries, not because this part is simple-minded but, rather, because this part knows profoundly who she is and why why why she is here. Nature's justification is the aphrodisiac for all doubters. That crucial time of pregnancy and the first year of a child's life is the most demanding, yet the most settling for an attentive and not overly distracted woman. When children get older than a year, the world seeps in and thwarts the pure connection between parent and offspring. In quiet times, often when putting Peter to bed, we come together and taste the intimacy between us again. Is this what binds families? Parents to their children? I want to remember these times. It is important to document this brief journey through belonging because it doesn't last. I can feel it waning already, tugged by my returning ambition and her yearning for independence. I want to rage, to block the door with huge granite boulders. Instead, I bow gracefully like the stem of a tall flower. Where is the next resting place for my soul? It seems a long and worldly stretch before me. Will death one day seem as inviting as giving birth? I don't know.

September 12

Parenting is a public art. There is an immediate, felt intimacy between parents. Just as people at a rally for some social cause feel a rush of kinship with those around them, parents can exchange conspiratorial nods from across restaurants or just while crossing other's paths while walking. Encounters make us critics and sympathizers both in a most careful balancing of opinions, condolences, and confessions. Banter at the playground or in the cafeteria of some sterile shopping mall leaves us deeply touched at times and put off at others.

Today I stood in the park with my son as a woman with two small, pre-school-aged children and one toddler walked up and joined us. Melisande was soundly asleep in her stroller at my side and Peter was climbing the slide. Through conversation it was established that the young girl was hers and that this mother baby-sat for the other two everyday to support herself going through school. She confided in me that this morning, when strapping the little boy in a car seat in her car, her young daughter wandered away from the car into the street, stopping traffic in both directions. She said how humiliated she felt as the drivers watched her retrieve her girl. She said she felt like such a bad mother, and that she cried when thinking of what might have happened. I tried to soothe her with the comment that things just like that have happened to me, and that we're all just human. It seemed to me that in that moment a real warmth passed between us. Her daughter started off towards the swing so our conversation was put on hold. After catching Peter a few more times as he slid down the slide in glee, I noticed the older girl tugging her younger brother to the bank of the creek that tightly borders the play area. The incline of the drop-off is such that I thought he might slide right down into the rushing mountain stream if he lost his footing at all. Their baby-sitter, the mother with whom I was speaking, had her back to them putting her own daughter in a swing. Waiting till the last moment I felt was safe, I finally had to warn the older sister, which, of course, caught the attention of the woman. She looked horrified that such a danger had passed her attention. She rushed to the two children at the creek carrying her own girl under her arm. I wanted to say something that would reestablish our connection, but it was not to happen. She whisked all the children away, firmly reprimanding the older sister. I watched her departure hoping for the opportunity to wave warmly or give a kind good-bye. She never looked back.

That could just as easily have been me on that side of perceived neglect. None of us is capable of faultless attention with a multiple focus. Once those babies are up and running, they are capable of pursuing their slightest whim at a moment's notice. My friend told me a story of a woman who answered the doorbell to find two police officers standing at her door with stern expressions on their faces. One officer asked her if she knew where her children were. She said yes, that one was up in her room, and that the other two were in the fenced-in back yard playing in the sandbox. The officer then told her that a neighbor had called the police because her two young boys were hiding behind her car throwing rocks at cars that drove by. Exhausted and defeated she asked, "What do you expect me to do? Watch them twenty-four hours a day?" I can completely identify with her incredulous plea! Incredible as it may seem, yes, that is exactly what is expected. This parenting gig seems like a total set-up for failure, a sometimes impossible task.

September 13

Two days ago I was convinced I was pregnant, but the last two days I have felt quite convinced that I am not. The ping-pong game of wondering is entertaining and titillating enough, but I am ready to turn my attention back inward on my singularity. This doubling and partnering of mother to child holds loneliness at bay but does not address the truest state of us humans here on earth. Even though Peter hugs my knee and Melisande rests on my hip, I am still just myself, myself in relation to others. Time in a hot bath alone on an afternoon, I regard my limbs and torso through the slightly bubbled water on a gray, overcast day. How pleasing it is to be restored. I find my human condition as I am experiencing it to be interesting. I feel privileged to be able to teach, to have time and the inclination to write, and that I have children and a mate to rigorously sift my spirit.

September 20

My two children and I are of three strong and separate wills but only one person's ability—mine, carrying out the desires of each. No wonder we are so often a screeching organism of frustration and tears. When this occurs, my nerves twist and prepare to snap just like a coiled wet towel in the hands of some smart aleck in the boy's locker room. I stop, take a deep unraveling breath and let it out in an obviously exaggerated "UUUUHHHHHGGGGG." Then I attempt some completely disjointed feat of pretending to tear my hair out of my head to distract my children from their decided misery. Deprivation is forgotten and, on those lucky times when this curve-ball method succeeds, delight ensues. Part of parenting is knowing your own and your children's patterns of misery, and where the escape hatch is. I've learned that if I get ten minutes lying down in my dark bedroom away from Peter and Melisande, I can restore my frazzled nerves. After an accidental bonk to the head, Peter needs to cry for about three minutes on my lap before I can introduce any diversion. Any sooner, and the backlash of tears can last up to five minutes. With Melisande, if I nurse her to sleep before she gets crabby, she goes down much more easily. Ah ha, it would appear there is some sense to this seeming chaos after all.

September 24

She Cried the Tears of an Uncompromising Lover:

Melisande and I lie between comforter and sheets with my goal being to nurse her down for a nap. She resists. She cries. She can smell an agenda on me. She knows I am anxious to sneak out of bed to go write, to have time to myself in the afternoon on an overcast Sunday made for sipping tea at my own lovely desk. It breaks her heart. I resist comforting her in my own frustrated self-righteousness. We wrestle each other's wills; hers being to have me stay with her, mine being to get some well-deserved time to myself. Finally I burn through my ego's perceived rights to the other side and find that I am hugging her fiercely and she is a bath of gleaming smiles. I am regarding her perfectly at that moment and she, the clearest person I know, knows that I am completely with her. She demands nothing less, and thereby continually cleans me. She's a tough drillmaster, an uncompromising lover. At her victories, of which there are many, she immerses herself shamelessly, with such pure glee that she won, that all her victims are soaked with gladness for her. There's no beating her. She's right, and that's her power.

October 1

Before leaping into a fit of crying or a barrage of demands, my children have never stopped to ask, "Is this a bad time for this? Should I get back to you later?" Tonight I feel weary. Taking care of small children feels like more of the same . . . the same requests for apple juice, the eroding whining that beats on my nerves, the drips of food I watch fall and then soak into my clothing, the same Winnie the Pooh movie I've seen hundreds of times, the weight of her buttocks on my leg and the accompanying sensations of spider veins popping out just beneath the surrounding skin. The young, fresh me is under a heavy net held down by the weight of children's needs. When dueling crying fits escalate to a crescendo, my impulse is to bolt. Then I feel the iron clamps close noisily around my ankles. My former methods of reacting to something offensive don't work. I have to actually pro-vide comfort and reassurance for the source of my misery. It feels like I'm eating my pride. It is an unpleasant swallow especially when mixed with my own inner critical voice reprimanding me, "They're just children." They don't have empathy—that assumes vast amounts of experience. They don't consider what I might be feeling. They need. If they suspect weakness in me, they do not back off so I can regather my wits. No, they attack that weak spot as if it were a defect in their own life support system.

Yesterday, downtown at the Pearl Street Mall, I told Peter it was time to go home. He protested defiantly. I tried to put a quick stop to his beginning routine of whining, and his defiance escalated. He avoided eye contact until finally he spun right into my face with a wet, rude, tongue-flapping fart noise. My vision narrowed in an instant, and I was burstingly full of indignation. The adrenaline gushed through my body choking off any rational commands to my body or mouth. I scoured my brain for options that came near to equal the offense rendered me. Then it hit me like a brick of bad news, "That's right! I don't hit my kid!" I now totally understand why we, as a society, have generally evolved towards this rule—because I have experienced that when I *would* spank or hit my child I:

1. have totally objectified this child as the enemy;

2. have so much adrenaline-strength in my body that I could crush an SUV.

In a sane moment, I wouldn't want anyone in my condition within a ten-block radius of my child. It gets back to what a friend of mine said on this subject, "It doesn't pay to hit your kids because you could never hit them hard enough to make it satisfying anyway." I know it's on the edge to joke about something like this, since there are so many children who do suffer through real physical abuse. However, it's not really a joke. I have been pushed to the point in my anger that I have had feelings that I imagine an abuser has. I have yearned to satisfy my rage. I wonder what it is that keeps me on the safe side. Is it my upbringing that has instilled boundaries of decency in me? I know I have that to thank, but also I have had to establish principles, make a very personal choice inside myself that no matter how angry my child's actions make me feel, I will never react with violent words or actions. I have to watch myself, catch myself, rule over that proud monster inhabiting me somewhere that I haven't yet scoured out. This reminds me of a favorite passage from *Jane Eyre*, "Laws and principles are not for the times when there is no temptation: they are for such moments as this, when body and soul rise in mutiny against their rigor."

October 2

Peter went on a long bike ride with JP. When he returned I called him to my side as I lay on the couch. "What did you see? Where did you go?" I ask him. With focused intent he explains, "The rocket was slippery." I have no idea to what he may be referring. JP turns the corner from the kitchen into the living room and explains that they rode the bike to Scott Carpenter Park and that a jungle gym in the shape of a rocket was wet and slippery. Peter nods his head in agreement to his dad's longhand account of their trip.

Peter remembers his hours, marks his days by how a weed smelled, how the bark of a tree felt in the palm of his hand, a plane he saw arching the sky. He has no generic categories in which to place his experiences, so each is alive and brand new.

October 3

Standing on a chair, I reach up and get a box from a high shelf in my bedroom closet. From the box I take a tan leather pair of ankle-high moccasins that button closed on the side. Putting the box back, I get down off the chair. I look at the soles of these old shoes and a flash of all the past I've covered wearing them lights before my mind. Sitting on the edge of our futon bed, it is still mostly dark in the room because my husband, my lover, my friend of seven years is still sleeping. I regard these mirage-making shoes in my hand, which I have had for 13 years now. They are more a part of me than this man who seems, perhaps, a stranger in comparison.

I got these shoes the summer after my graduation from high school when I tasted freedom for the first time, living in a big city with my older sister. I worked at the state fair selling moccasins with three guys, all a bit older than me, all named Mike, and constantly among us was the light, clever banter of flirtation. I wore these moccasins in my later college days with a pair of tight jeans patched on the backend with an American flag. Carla and I were a near mythical sight, both with our long blond hair, slim cool air, and knowledge of being desired. Other than one Halloween when I dressed as Robin Hood, the moccasins have been tucked away. And now I—the me of right now—have pulled them out of long-term memory storage because as a mother of two and wife of one, I want to keep from spending money on a new pair of leather house slippers. These will tide me over until I get paid for the one college class I teach between changing diapers and lying in the grass with my children. With the consideration of a CEO about to make a merger, I weigh the benefits of an ankle-high, fur-lined slipper that I would have to bend over to put on with both hands, to the easy but drafty alternative of a pair of slip-on, boiled wool Bavarian clogs that I could wear outdoors as well. Then with a slight flush of self-consciousness for what I have become, I feel the distant eyes of these shoe's previous owner, my self of a decade ago, upon me. I straighten up, arrange my still long hair and with chin up, look her in the eye. But she and I can only hold a stare for a few seconds before openly laughing with love for each other and congratulatory joy.

Yes, for now I will happily wear you, buskins of my traveled soul.

October 9

It becomes all too easy to skim across the top of life, running like the wide-toed Jesus Christ lizard, so fast over the water that my feet never sink. Chores and responsibilities become my excuse. I also lack the means, a tradition that perfectly suits me, and rituals that seem true and worthwhile. Wanting to feel deeply is not enough for its fruition. Then there are the postponements. Ah, when the children are grown I will experience life deeply. The result of this postponement is an itchy, unsatisfied residue that sometimes coats my days.

October 19

How Birth has felt to me:

Firstly, the birth of my birth son: The God of intestines, clay and ginger root (to name just a bit of creation) came to me in the dark and took me when I was still a young woman, apart from all other worldly diversions, and lead me to a pool of water. It said, "This is water," and I said, "Yes, I see that." Then when I truly least expected it, It submerged me completely in the life-giving liquid. I was terrified at first, gasping for breath, flailing and fighting, until a light of unearthly brilliance delivered me from my searing pain; Mother Mary came to me, speaking words of wisdom, "I know; this really hurts," she said. I felt baptized in relaxed acceptance. Emerging from the water I discarded my superficial disguises like a crumpled gown, I smiled warmly as I walked away wrapping myself in a blanket. I took nothing but the memory of the child's touch against my skin to treasure.

Secondly, the birth of my son, Peter: Then It came to me again, when I was older yet again, not expecting nor soliciting such a visit, and It took me to the waiting pool. It said, "This is water." And I said, "Yes, I have felt water." Down again deep under the water, this time roughly flung as a beast swallowed by some cruel hunter's trap. I saw no unearthly light of insight as I emerged, just a gasping wonder that I survived with my life. I ran away from the water, afraid to go back, but clutching my new child in both arms, my body hunched over.

Lastly, the birth of my daughter: A few years passed and the sharp edges of my memory faded. I grew nostalgic and found myself yearning for that immortalizing splash of soul-refreshment. Upon my own volition I walked to where I thought the pool was and said, "Yes." I lay back into its watery palms and floated, suspended in the pool. As I dreamily walked away with a beautiful baby girl in my arms, I said, quite satisfied, "Now I know water."

Decidedly complete and concluded with my searching, just today I was arrested mid-stride by a taunting voice that whispered, "This is water." It keeps presenting itself as an elusive trickle, yet powerful enough to wear away the stones of resistance.

What was it I thought I was going to accomplish? What was it I wanted to write? Where did just I want to go? Did I forget? I am a porous receptacle for this God's imagination. Am I yet submissive? No, I still resist. I am still lured on by the glitter of individual accomplishments even though I know they are all refractions from one light. Every day I need to resculpt my ego and put it in the kiln of God's will.

October 22

Love is an injection. Love shoots through the tissue with euphoric release. Love is visceral. Love is hungry. It needs to be fed and reassured continually.

November 1

Sleeping with Melisande won't last forever so I hold her closer every night. She's beginning to crawl. Soon she may be falling out of our bed with no walls. She doesn't know that I am considering when she will sleep in a crib alone. I don't want to worry her with my pondering.

She wants me most of all. When others hold her she furrows her brows and coos a small worried sound, while obviously pushing away from any torso that isn't mine. Secretly, I lavish in her loyalty. In my den of inner desires, I want her only for myself. She knows me so well. She sees through my words—which she may or may not understand—into the very heart of me. If I am feeling impatient as she tarries before being nursed to sleep, she cries a piercing heartbroken cry and lashes into my eyes with her steady gaze. She expects so much. She needs me all the time. She uses me up completely, and I'm completed.

It's like the feel of new romantic love, when a brush of your new lover's hand against yours can send ecstasy tingling through your arm and up into your shoulder and neck. Those first few months of falling in love, if filled with sufficient fireworks, seem a bright enough source to illuminate an ever deepening bond, growing more rooted and secure, and thus, more tolerant of diversions from itself. Of course that beginning level of intense togetherness can never be sustained in this human world. It's too demanding to endure, too needy to tolerate forever. The compensation for the lessening intensity seems to be the deepening of the bond and the trust between the two. We can always touch back to that place of intense passion, usually through physical intimacy, and taste it just as strongly. So it is with Melisande, as our bond of love deepens, so too, life will intervene more and more.

November 2

On Art:

Life is long. Art is the nectar. Art is the expression of the juicy bits, the glimpse of eternity that comes after years of repetition. Art is a small cup of syrup collected from a forest of maple trees. I do not spend my entire life creating art, but it takes my whole life from which to create my art.

November 3

I want to record my happiness. I want a record of this simple time when my two small children hardly stray from beneath my wings in my nest, and I have a partner of my soul, a man whom I inhale into my body, mind, and soul. When I was young and surrounded on all sides by others like me, strong and unmarred, I did not question that I would live a full life as did my mother's mother and my father's father. But as I age, even just to thirty years or so, a few begin to fall into mortal failings. The shield of "other" begins to have gaps as I glimpse untimely tragedies. A girl a year older than I who was so talented in all the high school plays, with whom I drove to play practice and against whom I compared myself, has lung cancer. She is alone, divorced, displaced in some California town away from family and the friends who really know her.

Heart valves deteriorating, car crashes, freak accidents, these things happen to people I know. We play the game of probabilities each time we get into our cars or even just continue to live. Some statistician working for the insurance company we pay has already determined how likely our demise is because of car crash, bodily breakdown, or house fire, and is presently, thank God, hoping we prosper unharmed and able to pay. If only we could pay them to tip the odds in our favor—now that would be a service, bribing the actuary to lie to fate.

I am ferociously possessive of my small lot of happiness. I know there are other people richer, more successful, better looking, but I don't care. I know the future holds trials and sorrows for me. Right now I love my specific happiness and want to hold it in my grasped hands tightly, begrudgingly allowing just enough gaps to give it air to breathe.

I need to record this insular time of happiness. I want to preserve a glimmer of this feeling so that I can remember it when things change. I am not being fatalistic nor do I overly fear loss. I simply know that things alive continue to evolve. I cannot write of happiness when I am in a state of yearning for it. Then it would be laced with the sadness of my perspective.

My world is kind and joyful. My world is one in which possibilities are hatching and their amazed eyes are those through which I see my days. In my world a sensual dialogue constantly turns, pulls, and massages me in a fluid, improvised dance.

November 7

A tiny crab in a black corduroy dress followed me into the bathroom.

November 12

I grew up with such readings as, "And God so loved the world. . . ." And now I question, God so loved the world that It sent us onto an often hostile planet with limited vision, snipers, daisies, snow storms, mothers, fathers, snakes, bear traps, coal mines and faulty road maps? Maybe we just hope for benevolence in our God so we create it and defend our justifications. If you look around you in this world, evil does seem a near even force to goodness; disorder and chaos happen as much as order and growth. Evidence for reckless, abandoned anarchy abounds. A part of me can feel the desperate loneliness of being disappointed by the God I thought would comfort and protect me.

But, in that place in my heart where I "know" things to be true, I do believe there is a loving force responsible for this unfathomable beauty I experience. I believe this when I see a weed pushing its thistly bloom through a crack in a sidewalk more than when I see the most elaborate bouquet. Even though I rail against the limitations of this world, I adore the imperfection of it. There is a satisfaction to be found in the yearning for beauty and perfection that I believe to be more exquisite than saturation in either. *But,* you have to be human, *and* you have to throw your heart out on a line far into the unknowable sea of life. When you reel in your battered heart and cradle its pain, through your tears, your triumphs will have dimension and will be infinitely more beautiful for the scars they bear.

Dear God, thank you for this imperfect world, the opportunity to reach, and the space between the real and the ideal that makes travel possible.

November 20

Her beauty is intimidating. Her dignity is clear. She is perfectly direct. Her happiness transparent. The long, thin, curving strawberry blond hair that is tossed by the wind on her head combines with the pale blue robin's eggshell just beneath the surface of her peachy skin. She glows loveliness.

November 23

Children abhor weakness in their parents. I thought that to show I could not bear anymore whining or misery, I would give into my feelings of frustration and failure as a mother, and I cried in front of Peter. Immediately he stopped crying, critically regarded me in my state, seemingly withdrew all allegiance he may have ever felt for me, and yelled, "Dad?"

November 24

Back home for a visit in Wisconsin, I was nursing little Melisande at mom's dining room table where we always gather for our best talks. Amidst jovial banter, someone jokingly asked if I was going to be one of those Boulder hippy moms who nursed their babies till they went to school. I replied that I thought I'd at least cut her off by college. Joking around, such as this, almost always contains within it a very real offering of corrective criticism. A light serving of disapproval for prolonged nursing was being communicated. I wonder where that comes from in our society. I know a large part of it is just embarrassment over seeing a woman's breast, which seems to get flashed no matter how a mother tries to drape a blanket over her shoulder. Another source of discomfort is the investment of sexuality associated with breasts that people have a hard time combining with babies. The mental image of a wet nipple being sucked into the mouth of a baby who ferociously tugs and lunges into the feast is maybe too much for some people who've been trained in the ways of prudishness from a young age. Maybe it's just our society's squeamishness concerning bodily fluids. Maybe they suspect the mother is prolonging the nursing for her own pleasure, in which case they might be right, but then I need to ask, "What's wrong with that?" In the Toni Morrison book *Song of Solomon*, the main male character is nicknamed Milkman because someone "caught" his mother nursing him as an older toddler. There is a pervasive aura of shame around this label for him, a stigma he cannot shake throughout his entire life. It's almost as if a mother's nurturing, here in the form of breast-feeding, is seen as an emasculating force on a male child that left him "soft" and open to ridicule from other males.

That is most profoundly not the world in which I want to live. I intend to do my part to give breast-feeding a good name. For the sake of myself, my baby, and all the mothers and babies to come after me, I will nurse as long as I and my baby so desire. I will nurse my baby whenever and wherever she is hungry or in need of comfort. I claim this as our right.

Something To Do

Join or Form a Moms' Group

To relieve mother-doubts, discover better mommy-methods. and acknowledge any concerns regarding mothering, it helps to have a community of mothers with babes near the same age as yours, with whom you hold regular and relaxed counsel. The baby details of feeding, pooping, skin care, sleep patterns and breast feeding, are often burning within you and yearn to get spoken of with others who share your concerns. More intimate issues, like your sexual drive post-baby, also want to be aired in a safe and nurturing community. Even if you pride yourself on once having held sophisticated debates about politics in the Middle East, try not to look down on yourself for finding the details of diaper rash more tantalizing at this given moment. Mothering a young baby is more consuming than any other task most of us have ever encountered. The intellectual you will be back soon, or may even still be with you. Right now, allow the mother you, who passionately wants to take immaculate care of your baby, have her say. Beyond that, find just the right group of moms with whom she can share her say.

How to Find a Mothers' Group: It could be that there is a Mom's Group you could join that is already formed and going strong in your community. Check in the yellow pages for parenting centers, mothering groups, including La Leche League, and give them a call. Also, either the community hospital where you gave birth or the midwife who assisted your home birth may hold mother groups or know of one. Many times places of worship have meetings for new mothers that may be centered around prayer as well. If you're the outgoing type, you may even notice a cluster of moms meeting in your nearby park that you could approach and ask to join. Check notices on bulletin boards at local food markets or co-ops for announcements of mom meetings. Ask other people you know who are well connected within your community.

How to Form a Mothers' Group: If you are unable to find a group of mothers to join, then start your own. It's far easier than you may think. All you need to have in common is babies near the same age. Diversity of the mothers' lifestyles, ages, and personalities will only enrich your group. There are many inroads to forming a group. Try one that suits you and your situation best. Getting a friend to do this with you, of course, makes it much easier.

❖ Call the moms in your Lamaze class for a reunion and propose the idea of meeting regularly.

❖ Join a class specifically for new mothers, such as a yoga, exercise, or singing class, and ask if any others would like to meet afterwards for conversation.

❖ Post a flyer that announces your new Mothers Group. Consider including the following information: Fun and relaxed conversation with other new moms! For moms with babies ranging from about 6 months to a year, first meeting will be at (place) on (date) starting at (beginning time) until (ending time) and will meet regularly each week. Call (your name) at (your phone number) with questions! Hand these out to moms you see at a nearby park, your apartment building, your neighborhood, post it in your grocery store or baby consignment store, your place of worship, or a recreation center.

What to Do in Your Mothers' Group: In my experience, this is a situation in which the least amount of structure is best. Female conversation has its own way of meandering around everyone's individual concerns, so just let it flow. The first few meetings may seem somewhat superficial or timid, yet trust is being established, so stick with it and give it time. You may want to introduce a small amount of structure, such as a blessing for your children and yourselves as mothers at the beginning of each get-together. In one of my groups, we had a session where we each brought a short piece of writing, either original or not, and shared it aloud. The only tools needed are some baby toys and a few blankets to throw down on the grass in the park where you're meeting. If it's cold weather, you may want to meet at the children's section of the public library or take turns at each other's homes. Snacks and goodies are even optional, since watching over your little one is a consuming task, difficult to juggle with a mug of hot tea. Sometimes establishing a beginning time and an ending time for the meeting is a handy thing so participants can schedule their time accordingly. Meanwhile, just relax and let the conversation free flow.

Support Each Other's Commitment to Breast-Feeding: Continuing to breast-feed your babies is perhaps the best arena in which to support each other. Once your baby's legs start dangling off your lap when he's latched on, you'll most likely start to notice stares, disapproving glances, or questions as to when you are planning to wean junior from the breast. Practice your spirited comebacks, mother! "When we're both good and ready and not a moment sooner," might work. Don't cave in to society's silly presumption that extended breast-feeding is indecent or "unnatural." There is nothing more wholesome or natural than nourishing your baby, as God intended, with mother's milk. You may be surprised to learn that breast-feeding in public is against the law in many communities. In the spirit of Martin Luther King Jr., it is your duty, mother, to resist unjust laws. My friend, who is a midwife, has even held "nurse-ins" as a peaceful protest at establishments where a mother has been asked not to breast-feed in public.

On a smaller scale, talk with each other in your mother's group as to how you deal with the pressure from your extended family and friends around the subject of breast-feeding. Many family members want to curtail the longevity of nursing so they can feel closer to your baby and feed him. Believing that your child needs a large support community to thrive, find some other ways for aunties and mother-in-laws to feed your baby. Put some expressed milk or chamomile tea in a bottle or let her feed your baby his baby cereal. Pride and hurt feelings can get intertwined in this mild clash of interests. More than once, I found myself guilty of wanting to prolong my exclusive closeness with my baby through breast-feeding. Sharing your child with the world is the inevitable destination towards which this path of mothering is leading. Talk about it among your counsel of mothers. Find out how others navigated through this touchy terrain with family love intact. Admit to your negative feelings as a way of growing beyond them.

The Long-term Pay 0ff: Your fellow mothers group members will be a community of mothers with whom you will share an intimacy your entire lives. They knew you when you were tender, open, and just beginning as a mother. As witnesses, they have an investment in the well-being and continued happiness of your family. With them, you can celebrate achievements and share the weight of sorrows. Even if you drift apart or move to other cities, try to stay in touch, even if just through email or yearly reunions with those still living close. Being in community with people who know your story and cheer its successful outcome is a richness beyond measure.

Chapter Nine
Leaving Babyhood Behind: 10-12 months

What to watch for

What is Gained and What is Lost

Let's start with what has been gained—a list that could encompass the world, no doubt. First of all, you've been taken to your limits and have survived—no small feat. Through this experience you've most likely established some friendships with other mothers that may last you a lifetime. Nurture these and never doubt their worth. We women spin a nearly unseen web of filament during each of these connections, such that if any of our children (or we, ourselves) should chance to stumble, this safety net will be sure to break the fall. You've also gained a bond with your child that will serve as the rock-solid foundation upon which you will continue to build. Also gained is a view of the world from your child's perspective; thrills passé become new again. In this year of your child's life, you've also gained a bit more of your own independence, maybe even, dare I say it, time to yourself. As much as every mother treasures time with her child, solitude is a human hunger and a time during which wisdom can be distilled from all the input of experiences and sensations. You need time for reflection on all that has transpired through this pregnancy and the first year. Since it's uncertain that anyone else may offer this to you, be sure to make the effort to claim some time for yourself.

What is lost? Intimacy—that pure, unpolluted, uninterrupted intimacy is lost. It's not that it can't be revisited or captured in quiet moments together with your child, but it is not ever experienced again with the same intensity and purity. Even though there are delights to be had around each developmental corner, this near-divine intimacy that a mother experiences with her less-than-a-year-old child must be acknowledged, and its loss mourned. I don't believe we can truly step into our future until we have fully mourned our past. Go ahead and cry. Tuck a hanky up your sleeve. Surrender to nostalgia and sink deeply into its ocean. Don't worry about drowning, since there are still plenty of your child's immediate needs to pull you out again and thrust you back on shore.

Rebounding Acceptance

You may feel nothing short of amazement that your child loves and accepts you so fully, even given all your limitations, fumbles, and faults. In this gift can be found the abundant love to act in a like fashion. Inspired by that love, you can feel gratitude for what is given, forgiveness for what is lacking, and acceptance for what is. Being accepted by your child so much resembles self-acceptance (since it comes from within) that it seems to trigger a full-blown, self-accepting, invigorating peace at the very core of your being. Ruminate on this ember inside that can give off such warmth. Pull up a chair and sit by it every day to comfort your extremities made cold by a sometimes-indifferent world. Having been so blessed, share your mother-grace with our childlike world, which still very much seeks such reassurance and love.

Seeing Double

In the doubling of yourself, you have doubled your everything. A child is in the world who is flesh of your flesh, soul of your soul. Though not identical to you, save for the same arch in the nose and long skinny toes, more oxygen is being used up since you procreated. Now you have twice a stake in the future. You have twice the reason to care about the legacy our generation is handing down to the next, and twice the strength to make a difference. You have twice the accomplishments to cheer, twice the obstacles to conquer, twice the shoes to tie, twice the laughter and twice the tears. Nothing will ever be as carefree again nor will you likely suffer from lack of purpose. Having reached the highest summit of human achievement, you are sharing your prize with the world in hopes it greets your child with goodness. Seldom used adjectives such as "magnanimous" are being dusted off and placed in sentences preceding your name. If you feel twice as deeply and soar twice as high, then, indeed, you must be twice alive.

One Traveler's Journal

Thanksgiving

Cornucopia: (A tribute to the value of a really good friend)

You come over with your two children, whose small young lives are woven in a tangle of threads into my own mother shawl. We pool our assets to create a dinner of curries, hot dogs, rice, and peas. We stack children on top of pillows, dictionaries, then chairs, so they can reach this eclectic feast. Amid giggles and cries for milk, we feast, you and I, on each other's words, those words of each other's that we pull on like a lifeline, bringing us to the living pool of each other's thoughts. Throughout the week we tuck our experiences, those most poignant bits we have read from journals, lines we have eaves-dropped, all into the drawstring bag that we try to hold above the stampeding demands of children. Then we spill them on the table, and they, we, words, spiral upwards in a tornado of dialogue and belly laughs of recognition, all while feeding a frenzied farmyard of young'uns.

You read me a poem by Mary Oliver about the creative self within the many selves we are. The two older kids are outside and we are trying to lure the two younger into the window-paned tearoom where the toys are shelved. We lift our young tikes under the arms and deposit them in the room, animate the stuffed cow, hand it to the child who immediately notices that it is lifeless in her hands, and run back into the dining room where you read me a few nourishing illicit lines. "Creativity needs solitude; it needs time," you read. I swallow yearn-ingly. All too soon, first one and then the other small crawling child emerges from the play room towards us, one holding up a small plas-tic toy he cannot decipher, her reaching up to be held.

You say, "I don't think Mary Oliver had children."

I say, "Then what the hell does she know?" and we laugh, certain that we are very funny.

The two older kids come bursting in through the back door, threatening that they are bandits who are going to steal our babies. We each raise a considering eyebrow.

We come together to pool our food, our words, our children's laughter. The feast would be maddening for some, intolerable for others, but for you and me it is a soul-sustaining helping in a full course life.

December 14

Frazzled. My nerves are out past the border of my skin . . . shaky, on the edge. I feel self-consciously melodramatic lamenting the difficulty of getting around with two small children, as many people have managed much more. But right now I wish to push that knowledge to the side and announce that I am bushed and feeling overwhelmed, with not enough time to myself. I have been going along expecting too much from myself while making generous allowances for others. Now, uncensored, I need to claim more of myself. Self-conscious of sounding like a spoiled whiner, I convince myself I have a perfect life, which I nearly do have. As I broke down today in front of JP, I felt a nagging self-critical element behind me that left me feeling unworthy, or undeserving of a breakdown when other women have done much more. I hold myself up to the example of frontier women who gave birth in covered wagons, or single mothers who have to send their children off to day care, work all day, and contend with some needy ex-husband.

I think part of it is being around the constant persistence of a three-year-old who is sucking in information and experiences at light speed. A three-year-old talks *all the time*. A child at this age is so fresh and awake and hungry for information that I know each question deserves a thoughtful and patient response. Yet because of the inequity in developmental levels, I feel consumed into his stage because it is seemingly hooked into my dialogue with it. In addition, it is a lot having a still-nursing, clingy little girl attached to one of my two hips or lap at every given moment, unless I'm driving a car, in which case she is in the back seat crying. And did I mention I'm still not getting to sleep through the night?

I need a mossy dark cave, small, very small, with just enough room in it for me to curl up into a ball and hide. My sap ran dry; my branches became brittle before I even noticed my thirst. I cried and cried, and once I started I couldn't stop until the need, with its deep roots tugging out of my veins, had spoken of all its specifics. As I unleashed my own pain it dragged with it the pain of generations of women worked beyond their brink—women misunderstood by mates, and others who felt alone, afraid, or insane. It is a womanly thing to give, to nurture with the food from your own plate until your own hunger snaps back at you and you are left feeling hesitant, even unworthy, of asking for nourishment from others. I searched the tired eyes of my mate who came home from work to relieve his crumbled wife. I searched his eyes for understanding, hoping not to find fear or judgment. I found compassion, but I know others might not be in the same situation. My heart opened for that felt-pain across the ages.

There comes a time and a point when you have to just say to the rest of the suffering world, "I don't care how my suffering compares! This is my breakdown! When you have your breakdown, I will be the first to hold you up and carry some of your load." However, it is impossible to remain self-consciously aware of everyone else's suffering when you are trying to recover from your own.

December 16

It is night. In my darkened room, I am sitting on the end of my bed, my baby girl nursing on me—my baby girl who I still see as an extension of myself, my pure and gentle self. I am directly facing an open door in our bedroom that leads out to a small sunroom walled on three sides by French-paned windows from ceiling to floor. It is a time of great intimacy here in the dark where it is quiet, feeding her rich, drowsy milk. Looking out the windows in the sunroom, I mindlessly watch the college girls in the house across the street through their window. With a mild voyeur's curiosity I wonder what they are doing, what they are wearing, and if they going out tonight? It is a comfortable view, a welcome distraction. Then one girl emerges out onto the front porch. She turns on the porch light, a naked bulb that sends a harsh sliver of light through the open sunroom into my bedroom. Her light illuminates me. With absolutely no mind of the invasion, the girl smokes a cigarette, laughing with a friend who has joined her, smoke rising up to the light and dissipating. I am transformed from safe voyeur to lit object, my baby's and my insular world has been infiltrated. Our dark, hidden, bastion of intimacy has been found out and the world will just continue to pry open this crevice.

December 18

It is time for Melisande to sleep in her own bed. I have dreaded this day for my own selfish reasons (her bright face my first morning vision), and have not wanted her to feel rejected from my arms. It came on its own, this change. Unknowingly she was claiming her own need to fall asleep alone, to dream her own dreams. No matter how tightly we cling to the body of another—mother, lover, husband, brother, sister—we sleep alone, perhaps in preparation for dying alone.

I feel the blades of the scissors slicing through the flesh that was not entirely mine or hers, but ours. I mourn the cord that bound us beyond the time that birth separated us. Gracefully, I bow to the progression of her becoming her own individual.

How did I know, you ask? Last night I foolishly put her to bed two hours earlier than usual. At 1:00 A.M. she began wiggling awake in a peeved sort of persnickety way. This continued at intervals of fifteen to twenty minutes throughout the night. If she moved, I would wake up. If I shifted my weight even in the slightest, she would wake up, and she would fuss. Nearly mad with sleep deprivation, at 4:00 A.M. I sprang out of bed, jumping up and down on the floor yelling, "I can't take it! This is like Chinese water torture!" I knew it was time. The next night she would sleep in a crib.

Though she has been in the world for quite some time, she has still been existing under a protective umbrella of my constant presence, within arm's reach. A discontented *coo* was all it took for me to be right there. Perched on my hip with one of my arms around her, she has viewed the world as though a marsupial with my spread fingers the pouch around her. But now she is changing. She holds her head more confidently, chin up, eyes searching with an intent interest in all that is occurring around her. Now when I hold her on my hip she sometimes pushes away, wanting to go down onto the floor and crawl across the terrain herself. Now my joy is in her discoveries of grass between her fingers or the cat's tail brushing her cheek.

I defend the dramatic nature with which I describe these changes. Please attempt to absorb my description of her as one needing me. She used me completely and, thus, blocked the longing urges of my human heart for a time. When I held her to my chest, she was a band-age for that gaping wound of individuality with which we all fumble through this world. I know this had to be temporary, but it was near heaven on earth. It was near perfect union. And as she moves away from me, in the most natural and healthy way, the knowledge of my solitary existence snaps back at me like a stinging rubber band. I smile. Yes, I know this is how we travel. I am strong. I'll be fine. But deep in my heart where this feeling is strong enough to weep, I miss her.

December 19

Last night I dreamt that my mate, my children, and I lived in a wonderful old house not even one city block from the edge of the water. In the dream I was determined to go to the water that morning. It seemed a large endeavor even though it was so close. I gathered our two children, got them dressed warmly for this overcast morning, and set out walking, holding both their hands. The edge of the water, strewn with rocks to step onto, was wonderful and once I crouched down near it, the strangest little fish swam to meet my fingers that gingerly touched the water. One fish, which was accompanied by many of her babies, was light gray and fleshy to the touch. Her face smiled like an Eskimo and I was greatly charmed by her. Then from outside my dream Peter did his vocal impersonation of a whistle from the top of the stairs heralding the beginning of a new day.

As I shuffled about the kitchen this morning, I reflected on this dream, the edge of the water, the amazing little fish so eager to meet me. This past weekend I had gone to hear Lawrence Vanderpost, a Jungian dream scholar, who told African San stories about stars and wonderment. I pondered the possible meanings of this dream. Living with children, their minds full of stories and imagined adventures, is like living on the edge of a sea of wonderment. Do I go to their water each day? Or do days, even weeks, slip by as I busy myself and forget to stop, listen, relax, engage, and be with them? I live less than a metaphoric block from wonderment. Perhaps, through this dream, I have been reminded to stroll to the edge and dip my fingers in often.

December 20

Regarding Snow:

Scuffing my heavy boots in the fresh light snow, I walk behind Peter. It is night. JP's in the kitchen with Melisande making a cherry pie. It is cold, but we are dressed very warmly, each with snow pants, coats, hats and mittens. I suppress my usual dominance over our direction and follow his three-year-old's instincts instead. We wander around our neighborhood that seems somehow brand new, freshly covered in a blanket of white, illuminated by street lamps. He watches his feet for a time, hunched over and then swings his arms up into the air declaring "What a beautifer day!" He lies on his back in a neighbor's front yard, the snow rendering property lines obsolete, and makes a snow angel. The night's purity of cold sky reflects perfectly off of him, no radiance lost. An angel in the snow, indeed. Rolling over, he lies tummy down on the snow and licks it up, not considering that snow might sneak in his arm cuffs or melt beneath his knees, or that he might reach dead grass and dirt before too long. His feast of the experience has no mind for etiquette, his napkin thrown to the wind as my pesky mind chases it down the street. This is why I have to follow him once in a while, to remember not to be too tidy with experiences.

December 21

I think we all want someone to take us completely. So often human interactions are timid advances and retreats approaching even exchanges. Maybe this is why so many of us are most nearly fulfilled by having children, because they take completely. There is no question, especially when they are young, of what is due or earned. They take. They take all day long and generously into the night.

When Melisande needs to nurse with all the drama reserved for divas of high operas, she opens her baby beak again and again while I fumble with my shirt and bra. When she can finally latch on she closes her eyes and leans into me with her full desire. Her consistent, rhythmic swallows seem to move through her whole body. She consumes me, and I, even though it is I who is giving, am fulfilled.

January 14

How parents watch:

As the balloon man on the mall twists and shapes a poodle out of a long squeaking tube of balloon I notice a reflex that has developed in me. I quickly turn my gaze to my child's face and watch what is occurring through her face. When we pass the man sitting on a bench athletically playing a Russian tune on his accordion, I squat beside her carriage and look at her face. I watch the music in her face. I must be searching for some remembrance of seeing things for the first time. Clever tricks of buskers no longer hold me in rapture, but I can get rapture from watching her consumption of the spectacle. She has the unabashed ability to stare someone directly in the eye. Since I have long lost that ability, I must see others reflected through her eyes. But far from complaining, double is the reward in this view of the world. Like windshield wipers on my jaded view, I see the world through her pure wonder. I get my first-time vision back.

January 25

Her singular obsession on whatever she spies at any given moment is intense and all consuming. Her triumph at wriggling out of the highchair waist strap to standing is complete; glee nearly squirts out of her eyes. A challenging confidence dances across her laughing face. She stands so tall she could stretch to the ceiling if not for the pink corduroy overalls containing her. While performing the slightest trick—a wave, a clap, a kiss—she gives a gushy glance to her audience, certain they will be in absolute awe. It is as though she has felt the first wind beneath her wings and descent is not even a possibility in her mind.

She is also experiencing her first fits of anger. When I block her from pulling Peter's shirt when he is sitting on my lap instead of her, she shakes her head with teeth clenched and slaps the air with her hands. If she sees that I am not on my knees before her begging forgiveness, she pushes out a cry with an artificially forced, too-sad expression that releases immediately when she looks at me again to see if I am repentant. If she sees that I am not impressed, she resorts to a lazy grumble and crawls off in search of other diversion.

February 1

As morning came, Melisande was already in our bed, rescued from her crib that stands six inches away. I held her in my arms close to my chest. My mind turned back to exactly one year earlier, her birthday, walking the halls in some well-worn maternity ward. My goal on that morning was to get her out. I wanted to see her, to be able to touch her and to regard her at a distance, with perspective.

On this morning I want her to melt back into my chest. No wonder growing up is so confusing and such a tangle of yearnings. As parents we alternately push them out into the world and then pull them back into ourselves.

February 3

Yesterday Melisande was crying for reasons I cannot remember. Peter, serious and deliberate, picked her up under the arms in an embrace and lifted her up onto one of our wooden chairs. Then he walked to a drawer and procured a paintbrush. With gentle strokes he painted her tears in swirls on her face. She was calm, quiet, seemed to understand. They continued this even after the last tear was used up. She would point to a place on her face and he would brush it with his brother strokes.

February 7

Poor Melisande is having a very hard week. She's afraid of her own shadow. It sticks to her like tar. She has seen that light can be eclipsed, that when she steps outside her protective home, darkness can creep up behind her in the image of her own shadow. The shadow of a tree or a building does not frighten her, just her own. When she sees her shadow, she freezes in that spot, stomps her feet in fright and cries out. It is such a real terror for her. I try such tricks as having my shadow wave to her shadow. I even get sidewalk chalk and try drawing a smiling face on her shadow, but she is not swayed from her conviction.

When I created her I had full knowledge of the fact that I couldn't protect her from darkness; some, but not all, and less and less as her years progress. Yet, she loves me and turns to me for comfort. And what do I, the god-like figure in her young life, provide without question? Of what am I capable? I give her love, my love as the purest, surest and most constant gift. Oddly enough, she doesn't seem to chastise me for my limitations. It seems the offering of love is enough of a boost to see her through finding her own passage into the light. She wants to do it herself. Perhaps she, in her time of clarity, recognizes this gift, love, as enough.

In like-spirit, modeled for me by my baby girl, I forgive you, God, for not delivering me from my suffering. Though I never fully realized it, my faith has been a tangle of confusion and resentment over what I could really expect from God. Now, as a co-parent, I can see God as a peer, the proto-parent, my ultimate mother, my father, and understand. I really dig the design you came up with, God. I love this parenting thing you started and all the challenges it brings to me. I like having real stakes for my actions and choices. God, I thank you for my freedom, your trust, and the chance to do it myself.

February 11

I end the account of her conception, incubation, and roughly her first year of life. It seems to be the time. This was intended to be an inner account of that private visit with life that mothers are privileged to experience, and Melisande has stretched too far into the outer, public world for this time to qualify. You don't need my eyes to see her anymore. This time seems to have taken both an eternity and the blink of an eye.

She is a prize to this world, and I offer her with a watchful hope that she will be met with kindness. She has a hidden beauty that seems always just on the brink of blossoming. She has a fickle, playful, spirit that will no doubt wreak havoc on a lover some day. Her gaze is strong and her connections into people direct. Her bangs are cut too short and her front tooth has already been chipped, but other than that she's near perfect, and I doubt anyone can deny her sublime elegance. I step back but keep watching on. It feeds my heart more than it breaks it to see her so grown up. So ring the highest bells and burst the barrels of the New Year's wine! Her spring is coming forth into the world. Plant a tree for her to climb, sing a song for her to hear. Add more beauty to this world for her sake and the sake of us all. She is among us.

> I have folded the laundry and am carrying it upstairs.
> She climbs the stairs above me.
> Sunlight spills down all around her.
> She looks back at me and smiles.
> I stand in her wake awed, simply awed.

Something To Do

Spread the Love to All the World's Children

Now is the time to celebrate your new ferocious Mama-grizzly-bear-heart and act beyond the needs of your own child, to the needs of all vulnerable children around the world. Though ensuring the health, education, and safety of all the world's children might sound like too big a job for some, with your expanded capacity, you're just the mom for the job. As you leave your insular world with your expanded awareness, it may be quite a shock to witness the discrepancy between how you are able to raise your child, and the conditions under which some mothers of the world must try to nurture theirs—without access to healthcare, clean water, education, or safety. This is no time to waste even a second feeling guilty, nor should guilt be your motivation. Let the solidarity of motherhood spur you to action. Look at this as a life-long commitment of love, just as you have committed a lifetime of love to your own child. Getting involved is your best bet for ensuring peace and prosperity for your child and the world community of which your child is inextricably a part. Beyond that, your spirit is allowed to remain open and breathing when you do not shut out the cries of those less fortunate.

Before I became consistently active, I often feared that I wouldn't be able to negotiate boundaries between my relatively abundant life and the unfathomable neediness of some of the world's population. That fear shriveled up and fell through the cracks when the greater focus of love shone down upon even my smallest actions. My fears only stayed large when I focused on them; once I changed my perspective, they appeared trivial in my peripheral vision. What dominated my vision was the excitement of possibilities, that I had the ability to actually bring about tangible change that would make better the lives of children and people I've never even met.

There are two ways to look at affecting change for those in need: first, through direct action and, second, through advocating for systematic justice. Both approaches are worthwhile and essential in bringing about lasting change, but you might find one to be more your calling than the other. Try to match your talents, qualities, and appetite with the form of assistance that suits you best.

❖ **Direct Action** includes efforts such as food banks, soup kitchens, women's shelters, and medical treatment facilities which offer immediate relief from suffering. The key to doing direct relief work is to integrate it into your new role as mother without compartmentalizing your volunteer work as necessarily separate. Be creative in discovering things you can do with your children. Indeed, the presence of your child may be the most healing thing you have to offer. Once a week my friend delivers lunches with her children for Meals on Wheels (a program that offers nutritious meals to low-income seniors), and it is the visit from her kids that these shut-in elderly recipients most value. For over two years now, my friend Juliana and I have led an art class once a month at a mental health outreach clubhouse, and we bring our children with us each time. In fact, it is the presence of the children that grants us all the permission to become child-like again in our artistic explorations. The obvious benefit of this, as well, is that you are engendering tolerance and compassion in your children. I have witnessed my son share his scissors so kindly with a mental health client during our art time, such that my mother heart was deeply touched. So put that baby in a backpack carrier and head for a soup kitchen. Visit a low-income nursing home with a group of your mother friends and sing nursery rhymes for your babies with the residents to the delight of all generations. Assist at a playgroup at a local women's shelter. Affect the world for the better and train the next generation of volunteers all in one simple act.

❖ **Systematic Justice** targets the systems of corporate and governmental policy that are often the root source of the very suffering that our direct assistance seeks to lessen. If working to improve the structure of government—through which we shape policies and map out our nation's priorities—is the thing that blows your skirt up, then you'll find ample opportunities to get involved. Just hop on line at your own computer or at a computer at a local public library (the librarian can help you find these sites if you are unfamiliar navigating through the web) and find out more about what you can do. Don't let intimidation slow you down; you don't have to be able to quote statistics to know what you value. You are smart enough right now to speak up for what you believe. Besides, these following websites offer excellent information to flesh out your understanding of issues and policies that effect children and families in need.

Children

Here's a collection of some of the best sources of information on children's well-being. Visit www.childrensdefense.org/links.asp for a more comprehensive list.

Leading the way:

Children's Defense Fund (www.childrensdefense.org), working since 1973 under the leadership of Marian Wright Edelman, has been advocating for all children in the United States The best place to find information about children's well-being in the United States

UNICEF (www.unicef.org), as a part of the United Nations, advocates for children in 158 countries and territories around the world. We all know UNICEF, but it's a site you have to visit to understand UNICEF's amazing impact. You name it, you'll find it here.

Save the Children (www.savethechildren.org) creates real and lasting change in the lives of children in need in the US and in over 43 countries around the world. Visit their website for information and lots of really beautiful pictures of children.

Global Action for Children (www.globalactionforchildren.org) is working to marshal the political will and financial resources to ensure, through community-based solutions, that all children have access to healthcare, education, nutrition and life-saving medicines.

Global Movement for Children (www.gmfc.org) is a world-wide movement of organizations, institutions, individuals, and children. It unites efforts to build a world fit for children. Read about the movement in six languages.

Mothers Acting Up (www.mothersactingup.org) is a movement to summon the gigantic political strength of mothers and others to ensure the health, education, and safety of every child, not just a privileged few. Find easy monthly actions to do and the education around these issues to know why they are so important.

Free the Children (www.freethechildren.org) was started by a 12-year-old boy in 1995 to free children from slavery, poverty, and exploitation. As an international network of children helping children on all levels, the organization is also freeing children and young people from the idea that they are powerless to bring about positive social change and to improve the lives of their peers.

Every Child Matters (www.everychildmatters.org) promotes the adoption of smart policies for children and families by making children's needs a national political priority. Visit their website for a free "I'm voting for Kids" bumper sticker!

Give Kids Good Schools (www.givekidsgoodschools.com) is an initiative of the Public Education Network working for safe schools, small class size, and quality teachers.

Kids Acting Up (www.kidsactingup.org) - join MAU kids in acting up.

Important initiatives to share:

Millennium Goals (www.undp.org/mdg/) are an ambitious agenda for reducing poverty and improving lives that world leaders agreed on at the Millennium Summit in September 2000. For each goal, one or more targets have been set, most for 2015, using 1990 as a benchmark.

The Convention of the Rights of the Child (www.unicef.org/crc/crc.htm) is the most universally accepted human rights instrument in history—it has been ratified by every country in the world except two (guess who? The United States of America and Somalia).

What You Need to Know to Truly Leave No Child Behind (www.cdfactioncouncil.org/2003_ActionGuide.pdf) is an action guide complete with stats, actions and moving words from many. You won't regret printing the 60 pages!

All the facts you need to speak powerfully to everyone (including your father-in-law):

UNICEF Monitoring the Situation of Children and Women (www.childinfo.org) is the place to find all the info you need to assess the state of the world's children. Great charts, graphs, etc.

How Well Do Your Members of Congress Protect Children? (www.cdfactioncouncil.org/scorecard2003.pdf) is a non-partisan scorecard for our Members of Congress. This is the best place to find out if you are voting for a wolf in sheep's clothing!!

Here's some great contact information to get you started!

Phone numbers to memorize:

The White House (ask for the comment line): (202) 456-1414
Capitol Switchboard (to call your US legislators): (202) 224-3121

To find your elected officials, information on voting and more:

www.vote-smart.org - everything you need to know to engage
in the political process
www.verifiedvoting.org - working to make sure everyone's vote
is counted
www.opensecrets.org - a non-partisan account of who's funding
whom
www.cdfactioncouncil.org/scorecard2003.pdf - a non-partisan
scorecard for members of Congress
www.grannyd.com - get involved in one of Granny D's voting
projects

www.rockthevote.org - empowering young people to change
their world

Federal government contacts:

www.whitehouse.gov - the President, VP, 1st Lady
www.senate.gov - US Senators
www.congress.gov - US Congress members
www.omb.gov - Office of Management and Budget (read your
budget here)
www.childstats.gov - federal and state statistics and reports on
children and their families
www.dod.gov - Department of Defense
www.epa.gov - Environmental Protection Agency

www.fda.gov - Food and Drug Administration
www.ed.gov - Department of Education
www.hhs.gov - Department of Health and Human Services

International bodies:

www.un.org - United Nations
www.icc-cpi.int - International Criminal Court

You may feel like a David poised against a Goliath, you may feel like your words fall upon a deaf world, you may fear that your cause will never triumph, but rest assured, "There is no chance of failing when one person raises her voice to bring dignity to another." These words were written by a mother, Stacy Carkonen, the night before she organized a Mothers Acting Up Mother's Day Parade to celebrate the rights of children. There is no winning or failing; there is just the evolution of becoming a fully compassionate member of the great human family. In that process it becomes quite clear, as members of the same family, that what is good for all is good for one. If that truth were to be unilaterally embraced, then the suffering caused by the selfishness of a few inflicted on the lives of many would cease to be. Until that time, let's keep our vision high, our hearts true and our hands ready to reach out to another. Let us find our sustaining strength in the undeniable truth that it brings more oxygen to a mother's soul to work towards a better world for all children.

Chapter Ten
Epilogue: The End of the Beginning and Beginning Again

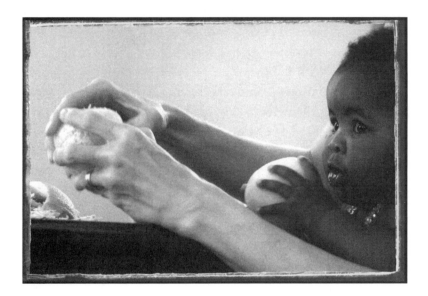

Conclusion: Eight Years Later

It is 9:00 in the morning and I am in my studio sitting at my desk to write. I have just returned from walking Peter, now eleven years old, and Melisande, just nine, to school. In a sling around my body is my newest baby girl, Lerato, only five months old and just adopted from South Africa. She is a rare beauty with her deep woody eyes and clear and generous spirit. Though we've only been with her for a few months, I feel like I know her so well already; and she, on her part, seems to know me, and calms when in my arms. To make up for the pregnancy and first months we missed with each other, I carry her on my body in slings and carriers as much as I can, close to my breath and beating heart. Adoption is such a different sort of spiritual gestation that I am only just beginning to understand it—a sequel in the making, no doubt. This one felt like more of a communal pregnancy, not just mine, even though I took care of most of the paperwork. Also, this beginning time with her as a "near-newborn" is not just mine. I have to share her much more, as the two older kids are head-over-heels in love with her and strong enough to carry her off in their own arms to goggle over on the couch. Even my husband is stiffer competition than he was with the first two, perhaps because I'm not nursing so he feels that he, not just I, can comfort her.

Before relaying the present-day bliss of mothering dear little Lerato, I wish to rewind to just after Melsiande's first year, to the mothering events that came between the first nine chapters of this book and the present day—experiences that prepared me for now and taught me true appreciation for the sweetness of this moment.

As Foster Mother

In the time that has elapsed between the end of the beginning and beginning again, a lot of water has passed under my mother bridge. Not all of it flowed smoothly. In the midst of happily rearing our two little children we invited into our home, through the foster program of Social Services, a teen-aged girl who had nowhere else to go. I had known Claudia (not her real name) all her life through a family connection. She moved in when Melisande was two and a half and stayed for about two years, though she was in juvenile detention and group homes during part of that time. At the age of fifteen and a half, when she came to us, she had already suffered more blows than most people encounter in a lifetime. Though we had known her since her childhood, we did not know how extreme her family situation was (this is not unusual, as most abusive families have very effective ways of hiding what is really going on). After her only parent—her mother—died, the details came to the surface.

My respect for Claudia's privacy prevents me from going into the details of that tumultuous time in her life with us. JP and I never regretted inviting Claudia into our home, but it ended up being a lot more than we ever imagined. Once she was living with us it would have been unthinkable to reject her. JP and I both tried our hardest to help her, despite our lack of experience. It was ultimately a humbling experience for us, and one from which we both learned more about the world of troubled teens than we ever imagined. The line from a Bob Dylan song would come back to me during that time like a mantra, "Come in, she said, I'll give you shelter from the storm." I couldn't heal her or even reach her completely, but I could give her a safe place from her storm. I never imagined that I was capable of doing more than that.

For me these two years with Claudia in our home were a crash course in some lessons I needed to learn, and a time of accelerated spiritual growth. I had always been wishy-washy about my personal boundaries, and had often allowed people to trespass on them out of guilt for having had such a good life myself. Since I had been so fortunate by comparison, I somehow thought it was my duty to take in the suffering of others. At the same time I lacked the saint-like purity to really do this effectively, and sometimes either grew to resent these people, or found myself judging their deficiencies. Not surprisingly, this didn't seem to help anyone, and it certainly wasn't bringing out the best in me.

Having gone through the *Claudia Period*, I lost that politeness that was a front for cowardice, and started speaking my truth to everyone in my life. Instead of sitting in compliance, I started to respond from my heart, compassionately but honestly. I think that for the people who really wanted to move on in their lives this was good; but for the others, who just wanted company while spinning their wheels . . . well, they stopped coming round.

I also learned that it's a mother's duty to expect and demand good treatment from her children—for her own sake and, more importantly, for the sake of her children. I know that this particular case was complicated by the fact that I wasn't actually the mother of this foster child, and also by issues of extreme abuse, loss, and mental illness. Yet still, I took from the experience a solid commitment within myself to expect and demand to be treated with respect and dignity by my children.

I will never know with certainty exactly how Claudia's presence affected our family. I know it contributed to the development of our kids' characters, and that they will be more compassionate, open-minded people for their entire lives. It made them a bit wise beyond their years without, I hope, robbing them of too much innocence. Till this day, when the kids count how many people there are in our immediate family, they include both Claudia, our foster daughter, and my birth-son, Ben. We all have much to learn from the unquestioning openness of kids.

The last gem I got from this experience is the freedom from some expectations. I learned that there will be people in my life from whom I should never expect emotional satisfaction. Some people will never view a situation from my point of view with my best interest in mind. I learned to accept this and be thankful for key people in my life from whom emotional satisfaction is a continual gift. I also experienced moving beyond the expectation of being recognized for my good acts and sacrifices. This has purified my act of giving in ways beyond measure.

As a footnote to this account our foster daughter, several years later, is now doing remarkably well. Sometimes just turning eighteen does wonders for a troubled teen. She's married, going to junior college, and has a job. When I visited a year ago, she presented me with half a dozen long-stemmed roses in the parking lot where we met for dinner. It was my first experience of feeling honored as a mother, and was an unexpected surprise as I had been nervous, before our meeting, that there would be tension between us. Best of all, I appreciated the love behind the gift and the easiness we shared during our lively dinner conversation. As she said when we were leaving, "This was just like old times except we didn't fight." If I were to look at that entire experience as a movie script, that dinner would be the last scene.

As Political Mother and the Creation of Mothers Acting Up

Although it was difficult being Claudia's foster-mother, taking her in had fulfilled my yearning for service beyond my family unit. After she left I wanted to fill the void, but I didn't want to jump into some demanding volunteer commitment too quickly without being sure that it was the best fit for my passions. So I gave it time. I began to do political actions with some close female friends—also mothers— who were involved in Results, a group that lobbies to end world hunger and poverty. We noticed that among us, our connection as mothers was primary. The act of mothering had led us to feel a commitment beyond our own children, to all children in our community, our nation, and around the world. This idea ignited our minds and we brainstormed ways to invite more mothers, who might be feeling the same way, into the political process where they could effect systematic change to better the lives of children around the world.

As a slightly clueless yet earnest first try, we organized an outdoor rally on a bitter cold, snowy December day, to be an occasion during which mothers could commit themselves to protecting all the world's children. Our closest friends came and shivered in support as we led the entire gathering in professing together our commitment to use our personal and political strength to protect children. After this pledge, together we listed, and had the crowd repeat, the name of every country in the world.

From this good-hearted attempt, we reworked our intentions and came up with an even better idea—stronger, faster, more spirited and focused. Mothers Acting Up was born, a movement to summon the gigantic political strength of mothers to ensure the health, education, and safety of every child, not just a privileged few. We launched our movement in 2002 on Mother's Day with a parade to celebrate and make visible this commitment.

One of us researched the origins of Mother's Day, and discovered just how auspicious our choice of that holiday was, and how harmonious our aims were with its founder's original intentions. Julia Ward Howe, best known for writing "The Battle Hymn of the Republic," called for a day in 1872 when the nation would honor that which mothers hold most dear, the lives of their children. She called for women to rise up and oppose war in all forms. About the Civil War she asked, "why do not the women of mankind interfere with these matters, to prevent the waste of life of which they alone bear and know the cost?" Howe attempted in her lifetime to gather a counsel of women to determine the means whereby the great human family could live in peace. Towards this aim, she challenged women to find what unites them over what divides them. Sadly, she was never able to achieve those dreams in her lifetime. Mother's Day was established as a national holiday a few years after her death, but soon became a watered down version of its original vision, void of its true intent.

We took dear Julia's simple yet profound words of wisdom deep into our hearts, saw the truly revolutionary implications of her aims, and used them to guide the formation of our movement. Moreover, we resurrected her holiday, made commercial and apolitical over the years, and infused it with a celebratory exuberance, inviting mothers to commit their personal and political strength to protecting children everywhere. During a breakfast date at our favorite diner, my friend Juliana and I created our visible symbol of MAU as a mother on stilts, showing her as a large and visible force in protecting children. This symbol became a reality in our first MAU Mother's Day Parade, when outrageously costumed mothers walking tall on stilts strode down the beautiful Pearl Street Mall in Boulder carrying banners and tooting kazoos. From a platform I, dressed up as Julia Ward Howe, read Howe's Mother's Day proclamation, "Arise all women of this day! Arise all people who have hearts! . . ." and then our MAU credo which goes as follows:

We recognize that we live in a world that does not prioritize or protect our children's well-being, and that this will not change until each one of us finds the courage and the strength to speak out on their behalf. Let us whisper this on the streets, yell it from our rooftops, declare it in our houses of government, "We will protect all children with our personal and political strength wherever they live on earth."

I invited all in attendance to commit at least one hour a month to doing political actions provided on our website, www.mothersactingup.org, thus bringing all our voices together, declaring to the governments and corporations of the world that we want children's well-being to be a top priority. To wrap it up we handed out new words to Julia's song, "The Battle Hymn of the Republic." Still a battle hymn, it now professed our commitment to the welfare of all children. As the crowd mingled afterwards we served delicious carrot cake, talked with people, and marveled at the successful outcome. I kept whispering incredulously to my fellow organizers, "People we don't even know came!"

By now, news of our website has spread like wildfire. It has become the backbone of our movement and an incredible tool for reaching out nationally and internationally to other concerned folks who likewise feel that the priorities of their government do not reflect their priorities, especially concerning children's welfare. Our website provides easy actions each month that specifically address some crisis facing children toward which our collective actions will most likely have the greatest effect. So far we have focused on issues such as cluster bombs in Iraq and their effect on children, allocating U.S funding for AIDS relief world-wide, and shifting fifteen percent of the U.S military budget towards programs that directly benefit children, thereby ensuring true homeland security. By increasing our membership we bring all our voices together to speak out on specific, timely issues and get noticed on the political radar screen due to our sheer numbers and the moral authority mothers possess.

A half a year after our first parade we posted a "Parade Packet" on our website that included an entire recipe for putting on a MAU parade in any community, from sample press releases to designs for stilts. We encouraged anyone who nibbled at the idea to email or call us to receive a flood of encouragement. The result was that just one year after the inception of MAU, eleven cities throughout the country, including New York, Los Angeles, Tampa Bay, Cincinnati, Albuquerque, and Vashon Island, WA hosted Mothers Acting Up Mother's Day Parades, to celebrate mothers claiming their voice to speak out for the rights of children. The courageous mothers who organized parades, several while still nursing babes, all overcame their own inhibitions to publicly declare their commitment to protect the world's children. It seems like the idea of MAU was one whose time was ripe. The number of participating cities continues to increase, thanks to some of the great regional and national media coverage we've received, even from *The New York Times*!

For me, personally, this movement and my involvement in it feel like a worthy and true fit for my passions and abilities. I trust and love the other women I am doing this with, and feel a life-long commitment to the goals towards which we are striving. I also like that this work feels constructive rather than reactionary, which is too often the case with political activism. As I, like most women, recoil from confrontational, negative approaches to politics, this celebratory and positive approach feels like a comfortable home for my budding activism. If I'm going to stand up and speak out for something, it has to be in a way that feels true for me or I just won't keep doing it. Anger can't sustain my commitment or interest, but the belief in every child's right to health, education, and safety can.

Reaching out into the world through MAU feels like a spiritual calling to the mother in me. It is cousin to the urge that cooks chicken soup for friends when loss strikes their lives, or the urge that wants to put my sweater around the shoulders of a cold child on the playground. My response to this particular world calling is a political one because, as I see it, the political arena, especially in America, is where the most far-reaching impacts on the quality of children's lives can be made. Whether or not babies in South Africa get the AIDS antiviral drug is based on a political decision to allocate aid to that country. Whether or not millions of U.S. children receive quality preschool through Headstart is a political decision. Politicians determine priorities for each nation's resources and allocate funds accordingly. Since no corporation stands to make a profit from lobbying for the health, education, and safety of every child, even the poorest of the poor, then I need to speak up and advocate on these children's behalf. Indeed, who else will give voice to the voiceless? Mothers are a natural lobby for children. The longer I mother and the more I identify myself as a mother, the larger my mother shawl becomes. I can feel it reaching its protective warmth around the entire world and the children within, and here's the unexpected pay-off: I am warmed ten-fold.

Mothering as a One-woman Show

Since the writing of *Twice Alive*, I have, of course, continued to heed my urge to write as a way of figuring out the meaning in all that transpires. As my kids began to age beyond toddlers, I noticed how the experiences about which I wrote began to take a more public form—how our family had strayed out of our insular world and were now dealing with real life issues. This was, of course, spurred on by our experience with our foster-daughter and by being a part of Mothers Acting Up. For example, I took them with me to a Million Mom March rally promoting gun control outside the theatre where Charleton Heston was giving a talk, and Peter had plenty of questions about all the issues at hand. Another time I showed up at a city council meeting with the kids to support the proposal for a larger and improved homeless shelter, and they were interested and engaged in the process. If fact, my actions were fed by my children's compassion for the homeless, as they never can pass a panhandler without insisting I give him money. The act of mothering was bringing on a deeper intensity of civic commitment and compelled my involvement outside of my little circle, not really out of any conscientious choice on my part, but as a natural evolution of my children's expanding awareness, and the greater freedom granted me by their maturity. I wrote in my journal about looking at these experiences through their reactions, and then wrote about how their reactions triggered new reactions from me, specific to being their mother.

One night in bed, I read some of these journal entries aloud to JP. Feeling the thrill of sharing them with someone else, I gave my reading some extra theatricality. I could tell he was moved and liked them. However, he felt that the words didn't belong on the page. He thought this material was begging to be performed, and that it would make a powerful script for me to present live. Taking his cue as an affirmation of my own secret, similar ambitions, and mixing it with my returning desire to perform, I started working on a script for a one-woman show that I eventually titled *The Mother Load.* I secured a two-week booking for the show six months out at the alternative performance season of the Boulder Museum of Contemporary Art. Then I got to work editing the material into a script. The script became eight different stories based on a series of real-life incidents around a unifying theme: mothering.

Though they all dealt with mothering, the pieces were quite diverse. They ranged from an intensely intimate description of how it feels for a mother in her baby's first year, to a piece questioning all the societal pressures that seek to tame the mother mind.

In the rehearsal process and in performance, I made it my goal to serve the written material. When creating something out of nothing, you have to ground yourself somewhere. Thus, the script was what I planted my feet in as I started to work. This was not an arbitrary choice, but one true to the fact that the written material was the very inspiration for the show. To keep pure the identity of my original artistic urge, I did not seek outside theatrical direction. I looked to the words themselves to see what they needed to reach an audience. I found that if I read through the script again and again while standing in a relaxed and ready stance, the impulse to move and give shape to the words would flow through me. This process demanded faith in the material and in myself as a creative agent capable of expression. When I reached a place in the rehearsal process where I needed feedback or ideas, I would usually just call upon one of my two most trusted and benevolent critics, my friend Juliana or my hubby, JP.

There is a recent tradition of women performance artists who purposefully direct themselves in their performance creations as an alternative to the model in which there is a director outside the action and the actual experience of the drama itself. My methodology seemed to match the subject of mothering since it is an enterprise directed by and starring the woman herself.

Getting my cleverness, my eagerness to please, and my desire to impress out of the way, I tried to make the performance naked in its honesty. Whenever I felt a disingenuous tone creep into my voice, I knew one of the three demons mentioned above was vying for control of the show. I wouldn't stop rehearsing or performing, but, rather, mindful of the obstacle, I would push through it, trying to veer back to the true course. The obvious metaphorical value of this entire process to life is enormous and carries a terrific pay-off. Achieving honesty in performance is accomplished by being truly present with the material in the task of communicating it to the audience. When this happens, I feel like a surfer who has caught a wave and is riding it through a limitless ocean. These moments are a high nearly unknown to this world, a time when I lose a sense of myself and am one with the ride.

I wondered how draining it would be to perform a two-hour, one-woman show—something I'd never before attempted. This is where the benefits of rigorous rehearsing paid off. I had built up the endurance over the months preceding and had benefited from the vocal exercises and strength I had gained. What I also found was that the clarity of my commitment to the work fueled my energy. Furthermore, performing is such a charge to the whole body and mind that energy from usually untapped resources keeps pumping through till the end when, after the final bow, there is a sudden crash and the performer is left exhausted and, in my case, prostrate on the floor backstage. At the end I felt like a water flask in the desert from which someone had just drunk the last drop, yet, ironically, I felt ridiculously exhilarated. Half of that feeling is relief, I'm sure, and the other half is the human joy of being used up completely to the best of one's ability. Also, communion of spirits in the holy shrine of the theatre is a high to which I am thoroughly addicted.

I also wondered how it would be performing such intimate material. Would it just be too weird to be face to face with a crowd of strangers telling of my intimate thoughts and personal experiences? What I found was that, given the practical demands of performing, I was left little room for self-consciousness over the material. As for my fear of feeling self-indulgent, I always knew that there was a higher aim, a common experience to all mothers that I was ultimately relaying through my personal stories. Also, the process of rehearsal naturally grants distance from the material, a distance that intermittently gets crossed during performance, such a strange flux between deep connection and surface skimming. The kids had their privacy issues around the content of this show, too. At one point when Peter was watching me rehearse this script, which largely focused on stories about him and Melisande, he declared that he didn't want me to talk about him in the performance. My heart sank, and I thought I was without a show. Upon relaying this to JP, he simply said that I should change the kid's names, which I did to Leo and Stella. Amazingly, everything was okay with them after that change, a fact that made me chuckle knowing that everyone in the audience would still figure out it was my own children of whom I spoke. The humorous note to this is that after opening night, when everyone was marveling over how much they enjoyed the show, Peter wanted me to change back to his name so he could get the credit for all the clever things he'd said.

Backstage before each show, hearing the buzz of conversation of the crowd, I would gather my disparate thoughts in prayer and ask that the gift of my performance be pure. I prayed that my offering would bring more light into the world through those who witnessed it. Self-doubt would sometimes creep in at this time, and I'd question if this show was actually any good at all. I mean, what was it? Was it even all that interesting? Since I had long ago lost the perspective necessary to answer those questions, I would just have to release my doubts with the acceptance that, good or bad, it was all I had to offer. Besides, it was too late to do anything about it minutes before curtain. Every human endeavor seems to demand faith most intensely at the moment just before it begins.

I went on to perform the show several more times in the Denver and Boulder area, and am planning my next performance in Chicago. It has been extremely gratifying to come to know my creation more intimately over time through sharing it with many audiences—like coming to know your child by seeing her through other's eyes. Though I have had some personally profound experiences while rehearsing, they don't compare to what happens in the electrically charged atmosphere of live performance. In rehearsal, I rigorously prepare myself and my performance to withstand the shock of connection that occurs when actually performing. In this exchange, I have to transcend the rigors of the performance and encompass the entire time span between the initial inspiration, the preparation of the material, and this particular moment in performance with all its quirks and needs. I have to be alive and present right now, with the audience in this moment. The alternative is pretending to see and be with them, thereby cutting myself off from any transference of energy, which, of course, is not satisfying for either party.

One of the things I liked best about this performance is that it brought together two formerly disparate threads in my life: activism and performing. My dream is that this show could be the source from which people might gain the inspiration to move from concern to action on their beliefs. The power of live performance can deeply penetrate defenses and barriers that defend inaction. My hope is that by exposing my questions, mistakes and struggle, I trace a literal map for the audience from situations of ignorance to a place of understanding. Though my path is not a universal fit for all occasions, I hope it is enough to start a dialogue within the audience member regarding the need for travel.

The Graduation of a Birth-mother

This year my birth son, Ben, turned eighteen. Over the years I have invested a lot of emotion in my belief that his eighteenth birthday would usher in a slightly new phase my in our relationship, as I have always planned to present him with my birth-mother journal at that time. This journal is a thick, three-ring binder in which I have written him letters, conveyed anecdotes from visits through the years, placed photos of him, stowed letters from his birth-father, and written a narrative of his beginning. Though I have always felt close to Ben as my "nephew," I've never openly spoken with him directly about the adoption. It's kind of an enormous subject to broach. It's not that we avoid it; it's just obvious and *there*, given that the adoption has always been completely open. We do kid about it, like when my sister-in-law, Teena, comments on how dreamy and artsy Ben is and then gives me a quick look and asks, "I wonder where he got that, hmmm?"

When my older brother, John and his wife, Teena, adopted Ben, they already had five kids and were expecting one more at the same time Ben was scheduled to arrive in this world. That made Ben a near-twin brother to the beautiful boy Teena gave birth to just nine days after Ben's birth. The arrangement has worked wonderfully, and was such a loving solution to an unexpected pregnancy. Neither my life nor my relationship with Luc was a suitable place for all that a new baby needs and deserves. I don't mean to gloss over this time as though it were an effortless transition. That taking of flesh from flesh was a trauma that hurt to the marrow of my bones. After the birth, I went back to college, living in an apartment with some friends. There were times in those first few months when I felt so profoundly alone in my despair that no one could really share it with me, nor did I care to try to explain it to anyone. But that didn't last. When I got my first few photos of Ben in the mail, looking at him made me swell with pride. At my parents' home that summer, I got to walk him down to the river across the street in the park and check him over, like a mother bird whose baby had fallen out of her nest and was briefly out of her care.

After Luc and I finally broke up, when Ben was about two, Luc moved back to Paris. Through the years Luc has communicated with John and Teena via letters, but has always been anxious for more contact with Ben. I have seen Ben over the years at family reunions, weddings, and during visits with John and Teena's family when they have visited Colorado. One time, when Ben was six and I was giving John and the kids a tour of our house, Ben tugged on his dad's shirt and said, "See dad? I told you she laughs a lot." I could have kissed him on the spot! Each visit is such an intense feeling of joy for me. If life were an almond, time spent with Ben is almond extract. I am extremely grateful for how openly John and Teena share the joy of him with me, and I am thankful for the easiness between Ben and myself. Even through some very difficult times, such as the death of Ben's dad, my brother, John, when Ben was twelve, this adoption plan has remained solid and been an amazing success.

So this December Ben turned eighteen. Ironically, this coincided with a difficult time in our attempt to adopt our South African baby girl, Lerato, with whom we were matched by our agency. Because our immigration approval had not yet come through, we thought we might lose our chance to adopt her. In the midst of a cloud of worry over that, I called Ben up on a snowy afternoon the day of his eighteenth birthday. Over the wires that reach across states, the kids and I sang "Happy Birthday" to him. I kidded him that he wasn't actually eighteen yet since he wasn't born until 10:30 in the night, a fact I bet he never even knew about himself. After chatting briefly about where he thought he might go to college next year, I told him that I was thinking of him two days before which was his actual due date. I told him that I loved him so so, so much. He seemed glad and a bit awkward, as any eighteen-year-old would. The conversation was a little shy but, I could tell, emotionally charged for both of us. After hanging up the phone, involuntary and unexpected sobs erupted from a recess of my being, from the place where I hold my love for Ben and the pain of having had to let him go. A raw sensation of loss clenched me as if he had just left my arms—as if no years, let alone eighteen, had passed. Partially it hurt because of how ferociously I love Ben and how little I get to express it. Then the pain from the possibility that we wouldn't get to adopt Lerato, and the pain of having had to let go of Ben when I was young, met over the decades and tore at my heart, ripping me from the past and the future.

A few weeks later, my whole crew drove to Ben's family town for his older sister's wedding. Because we are part of a huge extended family, gatherings such as weddings are very exciting, yet chaotic, affairs. This had always served as a convenient cover for me to make contact with Ben, free from too much voyeurism. My opportunity to talk with him came on the morning after the wedding, at a family brunch at Ben's house. JP, the kids, and I arrived from the hotel, me toting a heavy canvas bag containing the birth-mother journal and the five most important books I have ever read (*The Brothers Karamozov*, *The Satanic Verses*, *Jane Eyre*, *On the Road*, and *The Illuminated Rumi*) that I had long planned on giving to him. He was sitting in the family room just off the kitchen, where several other people were sitting around doing their own thing. I approached him, told him what was in the bag, handed it to him and said, "It's kind of heavy, in more ways than one," and smiled. He looked truly touched and thanked me. I also gave him a classical guitar, hand-crafted in Paris, that his birth-father, Luc, had wanted me to give him. Ben's grandfather on my sister-in-law's side watched on smiling, witnessing this exchange with approval. With that, I hugged Ben and went to get some food.

My son, Peter, stayed on with Ben and watched him as he fiddled with his new guitar.

As I spooned some fruit salad onto my plate, I felt the weight of silence lift off my being; the years of yearning to let him know the depth to which I loved him were relieved. I had handed over to Ben my heart revealed on paper, and trusted him to read it whenever he felt the whim or need. A calm peace came over me, and I felt content that he would know all that I wanted him to know about his beginning, about how it was a time of joy and not shame or sadness, that his life was celebrated from the very beginning even through the struggle. With each entry in the journal, he would read proof of all the times I thought of him through the years. With meticulous thoroughness, I had written about every thing that I could imagine he would wonder about. I wrote all about Luc, that wonderful, quirky Jazz musician birth-father of his in Paris, of his extended birth-family in Paris who all hope to meet him someday, and of my extreme willingness to travel there with him should he ever wish me to. I told him about how, even in my darkest hour, I never wanted to abort him. I told him stories about that sweet time when I carried him inside, of autumn walks down brick alleys to Lake Michigan. I told him the hilarious and touching antics of my labor and his birth with my amazing sister Pat as my birth coach, and how Luc flew in from Dallas and made it in time to hold my other hand through the birth.

As a birth-mother, I didn't get up in the night to change Ben's diapers or drive him to soccer practice, but I did actively hold him in concern. A part of my being was reserved, in an eighteen-year-vigil, for caring about his emotional, physical, and spiritual well-being. That monk like, cloistered part of my being was dedicated to channeling God's blessings upon him through my prayer. Now that he has successfully grown up to what society calls an adult, I feel a completion of sorts—that one chapter of worrying in my life is over, that a hurdle has been cleared, and a sigh of relief is in order. In the same sense there is a hope for a more open contact with him now that I have revealed so much of his story to him. Already, Luc emailed me to tell me that he and Ben are now in email contact, a fact that cheered me, especially for Luc's sake. I still hold out a slight hope for a trip to Paris with Teena, Ben, and myself, though from a young man's perspective, traveling for the first time to Paris with his mother and birth-mother in tow may not have the same appeal! In our defense, I must say that Teena and I are two exceptionally fun women, and should we ever cross the Atlantic together aimed at France, those Parisian jazz clubs wouldn't know what hit them.

Adoptive Mom

And now for the last mother installment—the golden coins (following a few storms) at the end of this long rainbow—the adoption of dear Lerato Mandalay Osnes from South Africa to deep in our hearts. I look down at her sleeping on my chest as I write this, and I am overwhelmed by gratitude for having her in my life. She is the balm that soothes all the old scars. She is my self-claimed prize for living and choosing well, for walking through rather than around the tests of fire life has set in my path. She is my passage again into the spiritual practice of taking immaculate care of a child. She is my constant companion and my renewal subscription to mothering. Mothering her deepens and makes real for me my commitment to speaking out for the rights of the world's children. As I consider all the indulgences this world offers, she is the prize that makes me feel a wealthy woman. Without each lesson learned, and without the self-confidence gained from all the preceding experiences, I never would have had the inner starch to ask for what I wanted in an adoption, nor would I have had the endurance to follow through the difficult path of adoption to its successful completion. Lord knows, I had to climb a mountain of obstacles with grace and agility to get this girl.

We started gestating the idea of adoption even before we got our teen-aged foster daughter. I had even made a call to Social Services to inquire about the possibility of adopting through them. I idealized adopting a darling little girl about a year old. Around this same time, a priest, whom I really like, gave a sermon about a parable in which a man went to sleep with his shoes pointing the direction in which he intended to travel the next day. However, during the night, God snuck into his tent and turned his shoes to the direction God wanted him to travel to do God's work. When our foster daughter came into our lives, I thought it was God being a trickster, taking my idealized yearning for a cute little girl and switching it in the night to a life-battered teen-age girl with nowhere else to turn. That may actually have been the case, but once Claudia left our home and moved to her home state, we clearly had an opening in our lives again for that initial yearning to adopt a baby. It took me quite a while to weigh my options and decipher my heart's true desires. I had just gotten back a significant chunk of my life as the kids had grown older and were attending school. I had a few itching desires built up that I wanted to satisfy before taking on another child. I wanted to write more, to dedicate more of myself to the college classes I taught, and I wanted to travel, using research on the performing arts as an excuse. After a year of more writing and class preparation, when Peter was eight and Melisande six years old, we took a month-long foray to Southeast Asia, visiting Myanmar (Burma) and Cambodia where we shot an educational video on the performing arts.

Upon returning from that trip we began the process of adoption in earnest. We visited pastel, teddy bear-decorated adoption agencies, talked with other adoptive parents, did research, and decided to go with a mixed-race program at a Denver adoption agency that had a fee price we could afford. Having worked with Social Services with our foster daughter, we were no longer interested in the route that seems to include a lot of uncertainty and risk for heartache. Since I am a birth-mother, and we had experience dealing with an at-risk teen-aged girl, we felt uniquely qualified to be successful adoptive parents in an open adoption, in which an open relationship is nurtured between the birth-parents, the child, and the adoptive parents. At the agency's request, we created a book about ourselves that included photos of our family and home, information on us, and an open letter from my husband and me separately to any birth-mother reading our book.

Then we waited for our agency to show our book to any birth-mothers in the mixed-race program to see if we would get picked. I know it seems a bit strange to have a mixed-race program separate from, for lack of a better phrase, the white baby program. Adoption is a strange terrain in which prejudices towards race, and the commodification of children, become very uncomfortable landmarks. Indeed, we had to face our own limitations, as every adoptive family must fill out a form listing what birth defects and what extent of drug use by the birth-mother during pregnancy we would accept. At one point while filling out the form, after having listed numerous defects to JP for our approval, all of which we agreed to take on, I asked aloud if we would take a child missing fingers or toes. He responded, half-kidding and a bit exasperated, "How many?"

We waited and waited as months and then a full year passed by without us getting picked. Feelings of doubt and disbelief in this process ever working began to sneak into my consciousness. Upon calling our agency I was assured that it was still possible, and that not many birth-mothers who would fit in the mixed-race program were looking for placements for their babies. I went on with my life trying to make the best of this time when I still had my freedom. It was during this time that I created and performed *The Mother Load*. The truth is that I spent a lot of this time day dreaming and having a hard time falling asleep at night thinking about a child out there growing in some unknown uterus that may end up in our lives. I had opened up a portal of my heart to invite admittance to a child, and that open space was letting in quite a draft and leaving me feeling cold and a bit empty. I never fully confided to anyone except my own journal how much the waiting was costing my being in terms of heartache and unfulfilled longing. I'm not sure if it was pride, embarrassment, or a combination of both that kept me from talking about the pain of not having been chosen. With these feelings only growing, another half-year passed without us getting picked.

Several of my very close friends, with whom I started Mothers Acting Up, went on a group trip for women to South Africa to bear witness to the AIDS pandemic and to do relief work. When they returned, they told JP and me about a woman they met there who had an orphanage and did adoptions to the United States. Feeling that our interest to adopt might be a better match in South Africa where there are so many orphans in need of homes, we switched to an agency in Georgia that did African adoptions, and within three months, early November, were matched with a two-month-old baby girl named Lerato. It helped that, in the meantime, we inherited some money from JP's wonderful father who had lived a good, full life and, unknowingly, left behind the financial resources to welcome another new member into the family.

Equivalent to a part-time job in time and energy, I worked on all the aspects of the adoption paperwork that needed to be done. We filed for approval with United States immigration, had to get our home study changed to fit international specifications, and took care of countless other smaller details that often required notarization or trips to Denver. It seemed like there were so many things that were just on the brink of going wrong and foiling our chance at this adoption. For instance, once our home study, done to international specifications, was completed and about to be sent to South Africa, the social worker at our agency said she found a police record on JP from twenty-three years ago for trespassing, and that the South African government might not like that. In a panic, I called JP at work and he, surprised to be reminded of such a distant memory, explained that when he was nineteen years old, he and a friend trespassed in a junkyard where his car had been towed to try to get the muffler off his own car for his friend to use. JP hadn't mentioned it because he had been reassured by the judge, at the time, that this offense would be removed from his record after a year of good behavior. The social worker understood and wrote a letter to the South African government explaining. Another time, when JP and I went to Denver to get our fingerprints taken, the agent who pressed my fingertips onto the photosensitive screen reprimanded me for having such dry skin and said that they (my finger tips) might not work. Incredulous and panicked, I pleaded with the rather bored public employee to let me put on more of her lotion and try again, which she begrudgingly did with success this time. Obstacles of this nature kept popping up, each time requiring me to wisely push, but not too hard, some public employee to stretch just a bit beyond the effort usually expended for each person with whom he or she dealt.

As it got to be near Christmas, we were still waiting on our immigration approval and were notified by the social worker in South Africa that if we didn't get it soon, the next family in line would adopt Lerato. This was despite the fact that our refrigerator was plastered with emailed photographs of Lerato that we said good morning to each day and kissed good night before bedtime. A deep ache entered my being. Unable to wait passively, I took to the phones and contacted each of my senators and representatives pleading with them to make inquiries and advocate on our behalf to immigration, which they did for the most part. Then came the torturous waiting. Increasing my anxiety was the knowledge that so much less work gets done in all offices, including immigration, during the holidays. With a dark cloud over my head, I tried to muster Christmas joy for the kids, but a corner of my thoughts was worrying about, or negotiating through, or hoping for, our immigration papers to arrive. That single and simple approval was the rock in the stream snagging us and holding us back from any more progress. Stuck, I watched with sadness as time kept flowing most persistently by us. The following is a journal entry from that time.

> *And I ask myself if I was a fool to have told anyone of our*
> *match with Lerato, but I have to think not because, though I*

*might have avoided the pain of having to tell people our bad
news, I will mourn and need support through this possible
loss. How would I get that comfort if I didn't share the
process along the way with those trusted people in my community? Having pain be a secret doesn't make it easier to
bear, on the contrary, it makes it all the more painful.
Supposedly saving face or maintenance of pride is little comfort and cannot compare with the healing power of having
loved ones help carry your sorrow to lessen its weight. I am
so poignantly aware of my need for other's comfort at this
time. Over-saturated, my sadness has spilled over my limit,
and I need someone to mop me off the floor.*

Another entry days later:

*One of my children, a child I ache to hold and care for, is on
the other side of the world, so far away, and I can't get to her.
I have cried on and off nearly all day. Tonight as I stood up
to go to bed, I felt like a person before a firing squad just a
moment after all their well-aimed bullets had torn through
my torso, leaving me perforated, blown apart, a bit numb, yet
chilled by the cold wind blowing through me. I felt a bit distant from my own pain, and was left wondering why I was
still standing when I felt dead.*

Then, on January 2, JP went out to shovel the snow off the sidewalk, returned with an opened letter, and announced, "Looks like
we're going to Africa." As a yelp of joy escaped me, I scoured through
the language of the letter to make sure it was the approval we needed,
and it was. A week later, JP, the kids, and I were in a plane headed for
South Africa. I am amazed that enormous events in life, such as the
adoption of a child, can hinge upon the whim of some government
employee who either picks up and deals with your one piece of paper
or doesn't. And what of all those people, with whom I feel a new-
found solidarity, who packed the waiting room at the main Denver
immigration office, each with a story, a dream, and hopes for their
family? Sometimes it seems unbearable that life is so tenuous. At other

times, this realization reminds me to hold this life lightly, not to get too attached to the drama of it all, to trust and, most importantly, to hold all in compassion along the way.

When we finally arrived in Durban from Johannesburg and were handed dear Lerato, who seemed familiar and small all at once, I remember saying, "Oh, she's still so small," and "I love her already." We passed her around and that night slept with her in our room in a crib right next to our bed. Since we resided in an extra bedroom in Lerato's group home, we got to be with her all the time instead of just visiting her for a few hours a day until the adoption was legal. Having her grow accustomed to us in her own familiar environment was such a luxury. JP was an incredibly good sport, living for two weeks in a veritable bath of estrogen, what with the six other female babies, their four female Zulu caretakers and all the various teenaged girls and women who came and went volunteering at the house. One of the babies, Sonya, was afraid of JP at the beginning, since she had been severely abused by her father, but by the end of our stay, sat on JP's lap and delighted in the bites of his breakfast he would share with her. Our two older kids played endless games with the other kids in the house, and thoroughly enjoyed our daily walks to the Indian Ocean to play at the shore.

This time felt like an adoption honeymoon. We had people taking care of our cleaning, cooking, laundry, and scheduling, leaving us free to travel through our days like an improvisational dance of "getting to know you." Lerato's needs and whims rode as if on a wave into this ocean of time, and we, the happy sea gazers, delighted in satisfying each one. It's as if we came to this adoption like a marriage of old, chaste, physical strangers brought together by matchmakers. Shyly at first, eager and excited, we came closer. It was a situation of total emersion, no incremental entering into this love affair. It was a honeymoon of five with all the possible combinations imaginable. One morning I walked into our bedroom to see JP and Melisande lying on the bed both facing in at Lerato between them, both of them marveling over her little expressions and vocalizations. At dawn early one morning, Peter crawled into bed with JP and me where Lerato was already asleep in my arms. Whispering, Peter asked me to put Lerato in his arms so he could hold her as she slept, which I did, and watched as he seemed to turn from a solid into a liquid ooze of love that formed itself around his sleeping little sister.

After legally adopting Lerato in the courts in Durban, we flew on a celebratory trip to Cape Town, then on to Johannesburg to hand in all her papers to the United States embassy to get Lerato's exit visa. This last stretch in which things could go wrong was so indicative of the entire adoptive process. That morning, after being stood up by the first taxi we had called to take us to the embassy, we called a second. He came promptly, but proceeded to get pulled over by the police who demanded we all get out of the car and show our papers. After giving us some trouble about Lerato's adoption paper looking like a copy instead of an original, as if he knew anything of these matters, they let us go with a shrug. Arriving at the Embassy, we saw outside the gate a line of over fifty people waiting that looked like it had been fermenting in the hot sun for a while. My nerves almost fried over being late for our appointment, I walked to the head of the line with an air of "important business" about me, straight up to the nervous looking African men with rifles who were guarding the embassy. My bluff worked and we were allowed in. The woman at the front counter looked through all our papers and asked "Do you have proof of her abandonment?" Inside I panicked, knowing I had no such proof, but still looked through my file of papers till I found a fax I received from my agency in the states mentioning that she was abandoned. I handed the sheet to the woman feigning confidence that this paper was, of course, all she would need. Oddly enough, it worked. Finally the director of the embassy, a bit of a good ol' boy Rugby playing sort, had us raise our right hand, swear to the truth of all we presented and said, "Congratulations and welcome . . . uh, to another dependent."

Once we got her visa in hand and were leaving the building, relief drained through me from my brain down through my limbs that had been so occupied holding all that tension, leaving me weak with relief. Lerato suddenly felt as heavy as a bag of cement in my arms, but ours, finally ours. Driving in the taxi later that day, I felt so grateful to be starting the mothering of another child. I see myself as a pot of mothering tea. I have poured out into two lovely children, but still have more inside me that I long to pour out into another cup of a child. Spurred on, perhaps, by the metaphor of tea, it hit me that I fiercely wanted to be home with her and yearned to do specific silly little things, like walk down to the Trident Café with her in the morning after dropping the kids off at school, or take her to church for the first time for everyone to meet her. I wanted all the people who love me, and have been praying and cheering for this adoption, to coo and wow over her. I wanted her to be a part of our home life and for her to feel it as her own.

Now that we are home, in some ways it feels like our family is just starting, as if we've just become ourselves. I love what the act of this adoption has done to each of us individually and collectively. JP seems light and funny, yet totally on target with loving this new girl and wanting her. Melisande seems inflated with self-confidence and purpose, dressing and holding Lerato or bouncing her on her knees. Peter seems soft and so deeply affected by his affectionate love for her. Together we feel complete, like we were meant to be, as if the potential we carried within us was realized. The choice of this adoption sets our family in a direction I want to travel with all my heart. I feel a warmth of contentment that I have not felt for a long time. I feel as if I have arrived and can truly begin the work I have prepared for all this time. Being the mother to a larger number of children makes my mother bird feathers ruffle out in pride. The affection and love it has unleashed for JP is immeasurable. Riding high, I feel like the luckiest woman in the world. And Lerato, dear little Lerato, seems to be blossoming in our adoring eyes as if our love is the spring's sun on her winter of being without a family of her own. She's getting a bit more demanding, timidly so, but growing more each day, just as every baby should (even babies in institutions who stop crying once so many of their cries go unheard—babies who learn to keep their needs to themselves).

In this way, Lerato has cracked me open like an egg to the suffering of children in this world. Though I had an intellectual, spiritual, and emotional commitment to these children before, now I feel as though I hold each one these children in my arms when I hold Lerato. Orphans in Africa are no longer statistics; they have names and faces for me, such as two-year-old Sonya with her gibberish talk and chubby waddle walk, little four-month-old Michelle who survived a near fatal brush with pneumonia, sweet five-month-old Yolanda with a halo of hair missing around her head, and little four-day-old Simtamba whose dying mother had given her up, the baby still waiting to be tested for AIDS, the disease that is ravaging their country.

When helping deliver food in a township outside of Johannesburg, we walked by a ten-year-old girl who was slumped on a stool outside a shack patched together from discarded, corrugated pieces of tin. Our friend, Cora, whom we were helping, told us that this girl had been raped by her father, who afterwards burned down their home and deserted her. It is a prevalent belief among uneducated South Africans that having sex with a virgin will cure a man from AIDS. Thus, now this girl, who already lost her mother to AIDS, is infected herself, likewise from her father. I was incredulous to learn that there is nearly no infrastructure at all in these sprawling townships, nothing but the water that gets delivered into metal storage units that children spend the better part of a day transporting to their shacks. How would a nation even disseminate aid, if they received it, when there is no knowledge of these people? They suffer with their dying in their homes, tending to them the best they can. The number of "child-led households" is staggering. Children as young as ten commonly nurse a dying mother or father, while tending to the needs of younger siblings.

I'm interested in how the extreme pain and suffering we learned of, witnessed, and opened our hearts to in South Africa is mixed with the intoxicating joy we feel in having Lerato in our lives. Strangely, this knowledge doesn't make me feel guilty in enjoying her so much. I hold it all in my heart, necessarily expanded by this experience. If I were a younger woman with less life experience, this contrast might have caused me trouble, but now I know that joy, when it comes, should be celebrated, especially when it comes from such adversity. I also trust that our concern for the plight of the African people is a part of us and something we are already acting upon.

> *In all of Africa, of course, it had to be you, dear Lerato, who came to us. You burst into us and exploded love into our little foursome making us a glorious and livesome fivesome. I wanted you so much. I wanted you across oceans and continents. Through sheer force of will, I bent the course of that bureaucratic vector such that they let us adopt you against all odds. Now you are in my arms through most of every day, and I never for a moment take it for granted. At times in our bedroom when I am rocking you to sleep, the gratitude swells up in me and spills out above my smiling face as tears of complete joy, and I shower your forehead with kisses. Sleep my dearest, till morning when I get another day with you. Yes, that is the ultimate gift, another day with you.*

An Apple a Day

I know that life will again have times of trial and sadness, that loss will strike as it always does in this naturally decaying world of ours. But this, most profoundly, is not that time. I'm not living in the shadow of fear because I have faced loss and have survived. There's no way to prepare for sadness except to live well and fully now, so that's just what I intend to do. A few years ago I had the privilege of hearing Archbishop Desmond Tutu, the Nobel laureate of South Africa, speak at the auditorium where JP is Technical Director. I was so surprised that a man who has lived through such extreme oppression and suffering had such a cheerful and light countenance. He was almost giddy, and somehow seemed above worry. With a twinkle in his eye, he looked at his audience and stated, "In my life I have seen incredible evil and I have seen extreme goodness, and guess what? Goodness always wins out in the end." There he stood, with apartheid abolished and freedom growing for every race in South Africa, physical proof that goodness prevails.

Faith that all of this is leading somewhere good makes it easier to navigate through the ups and downs. Awareness that life isn't always this simple only increases my appreciation for this immediate moment with my baby Lerato in my arms. I intend to bite deeply into this apple, this juicy flesh of the fruit that, of course, post-Eden, necessarily contains within it the knowledge of good and evil, of joy and loss. And isn't it interesting that we have dear Eve, our first mother, to thank for this courageous first bite. And why is it that our storytellers of mythological beginning chose to see this as a sin, rather than an invitation by God to be more God-like? Rather than seeing knowledge as evil, could we see it as sharing in the worries and the joy God bears? Expanded awareness is the natural result of mothering. Oh fleshy, seedy, red fruit of my desire and fulfillment both, how delicious you are. This is the only life I know and the one I have come to love. Thanks, Eve. I wouldn't have it any other way.

Footnotes:

From Chapter One

Gibran, Kahlil. 2000. *The Prophet*. New York: Alfred A. Knopf, page 19.

From Chapter Four

Hass, Robert. 1996. *Sun Under Wood*. Hopewell, NJ: The Ecco Press, page 74.

From Chapter Eight

Bronte, Charlotte. *Jane Eyre*. 1982. New York: New American Library, page 319.

From Chapter Nine

Osnes, Beth. "Cornucopia." *Mothering* (September-October, 2000), page 76.

Chapter Ten

Richards, Laura E., and Mary Howe Elliot. 1925. *Julia Ward Howe*. Boston and New York: Houghton Mifflin Company, The Riverside Press Cambridge, page 159.

Photo Credits

Chapter One: JP Osnes
Chapter Two: Juliana Forbes
Chapter Three: Chip Isenhart
Chapter Four: Chip Isenhart
Chapter Fife: JP Osnes
Chapter Six: Beth Osnes
Chapter Seven: Jeneen Osnes
Chapter Eight: Beth Osnes
Chapter Nine: Jeneen Osnes
Chapter Ten: Robynn Butler
End photo: Jeneen Osnes
Back cover: Michael Worobec

Something to Do (pages to fill with notes, insights, ideas)

Something to Do

Something to Do

Something to Do